This edition
has been limited to
2,500 numbered copies
of which this is
No. *188*

To Mark
very best wishes
Alan [signature]

Celebration of the Somerset & Dorset Railway

SOMERSET & DORSET JOINT R^{ly}

BATH

Midford

Wellow

SHOSCOMBE & SINGLE HILL HALT

Midsomer Norton

Radstock

Chilcompton

BURNHAM

HIGHBRIDGE

Bason Bridge

Edington Jct

Shapwick

Ashcott

BAWDRIP HALT

Cossington

BRIDGWATER

Binegar

Masbury

WELLS

Polsham

Shepton Mallet

Evercreech New

GLASTONBURY

West Pennard

Pylle

EVERCREECH Jct

Cole

Wincanton

TEMPLECOMBE

Henstridge

Stalbridge

Sturminster Newton

Shillingstone

STOURPAINE & DURWESTON HALT

Blandford Forum

CHARLTON MARSHALL HALT

Spetisbury

Bailey Gate

CORFE MULLEN HALT

Broadstone

CREEKMOOR HALT

WIMBORNE

Poole

Parkstone

Branksome

BOURNEMOUTH

Illustrated by Duncan Harper

Celebration of the
Somerset & Dorset Railway

Alan Hammond

Millstream Books

I would like to dedicate this book to Keith Barrett who is a former S&D fireman and a very good friend. Over the years he has given me enormous amounts of help and encouragement with my books and has allowed me to use many of his photographs from his own private collection. With his vast knowledge and memories of the railway, he has put me right on many occasions. Keith is a Somerset & Dorset railwayman through and through and it is a privilege to know him.

The map which appears as the frontispiece to this book is available as a print at the same size for the post-inclusive price of £2.50 from Millstream Books, 18 The Tyning, Bath BA2 6AL

First published in 2006 by
Millstream Books, 18 The Tyning, Bath BA2 6AL

Set in Times New Roman and printed in Great Britain by
The Amadeus Press, Cleckheaton, West Yorkshire

© Alan Hammond 2006

ISBN 0 948975 76 8

British Library Cataloguing-in-Publication Data:
a catalogue record for this book is available from the British Library

Foreword

I am very pleased to write this foreword for Alan's new book *Celebration of the Somerset & Dorset Railway*. The year 2006 is very special for both of us for different reasons.

I was brought up in Farnworth, Bolton where a sense of family unity was very important for all generations. I am sure this would be the same for the Somerset & Dorset Railway families. We had a station at Farnworth under the LMS banner, which went from Bolton to Manchester. As youngsters we would watch the steam engines go by with passenger and goods trains. At nine years old our family moved to Oswestry where the railway was part of the BR Western Region, it also had a railway works there.

My working life was as a professional footballer playing for such clubs as Everton, where we won the League Championship, Arsenal, Manchester City and Blackpool. I also played for England in two World Cups, and won over 70 caps for my country. After my playing career came to an end I managed various clubs which have included Portsmouth, Manchester City, Southampton and Stoke City.

Football is a team game and a railway like the S&D was also run by a team where everybody pulled together to get the end result.

I recall one important train journey when I went to sign for Arsenal from Everton. Other clubs were interested in signing me and one of them had a representative at Euston Station to talk to me. Arsenal found out about this and when the train reached Watford Junction, the last stop before Euston, the Arsenal secretary was on the platform looking out for me. Once he found me he suggested that if I got off the train now he would drive me to Highbury. This I did and duly signed for the Gunners.

I was very pleased to have my autobiography published recently, with James Mossop, called *Playing Extra Time* and I now know the amount of work that goes into writing a book.

Of course 2006 is a very special year for me; it was 40 years ago, when, as a member of the England World Cup team, we beat West Germany 4-2 after extra time at Wembley, to win the Jules Rimet Trophy. To win the World Cup for your country is something very special in your life. For Alan Hammond 2006 means the 40th anniversary of the end of the much loved Somerset & Dorset Railway. Alan's new book has turned the sorrow of this event into a celebration of memories and photographs. So if you enjoy steam with nostalgia this splendid book is a must for you.

Alan Ball, MBE

Introduction and Acknowledgements

It is 40 years since the S&D closed; much has been said and written about the circumstances of its demise. Maybe I have rose tinted glasses on, but I want to celebrate this railway and not remember its closure; hopefully you feel the same way. *Celebration of the Somerset & Dorset Railway* brings back to life those days when this unique railway was the life blood for so many people. Let us wend our way across the Mendips and head towards the sea at Bournemouth and Burnham with a selection of photographs and memories from staff, which hopefully whets your appetite for those bygone days of a special railway. In this volume I have concentrated on the memories of the young firemen who were firing engines over the Somerset & Dorset Railway at a very early age.

I would like to extend my sincere thanks to everyone who has helped with this publication. To my publisher, Tim Graham, for putting up with me on our ninth book together and his skills in designing this book. My very grateful thanks go to Alan Ball MBE for writing the foreword. To my wife and best friend, Christine, who is now an author in her own right; she has been a real star with her skills on cleaning and repairing many of the photographs and also making sure I press the right keys on the computer. Keith Barrett has again given me a great amount of advice and help in all aspects of the book including access to his collection of photographs.

Many thanks go to the contributors of the photographs and memories with a special mention to photographers Paul Strong, Alan Mitchard, Hugh Ballantyne and John Cornelius who have allowed me to use many of their superb shots. Andy Moon and Roy Pitman have again given me invaluable assistance for which I am very grateful. Tim Deacon has been really helpful with an updated list of staff, so important in a book like this. My grateful thanks go to the proof readers: Richard Derry, Christine Hammond, Allan Stanistreet, John Simms, Roy Pitman, Keith Barrett and Graham Hooper.

Many others have given me assistance with the book including The Somerset & Dorset Railway Trust, The Somerset & Dorset Railway Heritage Trust, North Dorset Railway Trust, Gartell Light Railway, Wally Moon, Bob Downes, Chris Handley, Richard Dagger, John Stamp, Arthur Turner, Gerry White, Ivor Willshire, Billy & Keith Conibeer, Pat Bean, Bill Harford, Percy Parsons, Mike Ryall, Wayne Mayo, Frank Kemp, George Welch, Barry Andrews, Fred Gapper, Len Taylor, Wally Arnott, Joan, Fred & Andrew Fisher, Maurice & Norman Cook, Gordon King, Dennis Ashill, John Thick, Ian Bunnett, Vic Freak, Gordon Webb, Mark Lambert, Max Shore, Rita Smart, Colin Jackson, David Strawbridge, George Tucker, Les & Mary Haines, Ron Hatcher, Julian Peters, Gerald Box, Mick Elliott, John Sawyer, David Walker, Len West, Keran A. Walden, Ralph Holden, Albert Parsons, Paul Guppy, Mike Rutter, Roger Raisey, Ken Stokes, Maureen Carroll, John Pearce, Bert Short, Mrs. M. Brown, Janet & Tony Rossiter, Brian Harding, Pat Holmes, Betty Spiller, John Eaton, Raymond Dunkerton, Fred Faulks, Ken Burston, Nigel Pass, Lesley Miles, Michael & Ruth Bishop, Alan Cox, Jim Milton, Ian Matthews, Alan Backhouse, John Dray, Alan Grieve, Robin Gould, Roy Hix, George Gillard, Ken Coffin, Edna & Jack Dulborough, Stuart Mullins, Colin Brine, Norman Brooks, John Curtis, Graham O'Donnell, Geoffrey Robinson and John Lancastle.

As many photographs are from people's collections, a reader may well recognise a photograph that they took. I offer my apologies in advance for not being able to credit you in person.

It is a poignant reminder that with the passing of 40 years since the S&D closed, we are sadly losing members of staff, and since my last book we have lost Ivor (Ginger) Ridout, Harold Moody, Roy Nancarrow, Trevor Jeans, Fred Parsons, Len West, Maurice Cook, Mike Ryall, Colin Powis, Norman Light, Tony Pitt and Charlie Pitt.

Outwood Common, Billericay, football team nearly 30 years ago, with me at the end on the right, kneeling down. It seems such a long time since I played for Ipswich Town Youth and semi-professional with Leyton, Rainham Town and Brentwood. Wouldn't it be lovely to turn the clock back for just one more game?

The Somerset & Dorset Railway: A Brief Historical Outline

John Simms

Looking back it seems that nothing was ever straightforward about the Somerset & Dorset Railway, from its origins as a short railway in Somerset to the last-minute extension of its life before final closure. The full tale has been told elsewhere, most notably by Robin Atthill. This is simply intended as a short summary of some main points.

The story begins with the Somerset Central Railway, which was promoted and built to link Glastonbury with the Bristol & Exeter Railway at Highbridge. It was also extended across the B&E to the wharf at Highbridge and to Burnham-on-Sea. Opened in 1854 and built to Brunel's broad gauge it was further extended to Wells and then work began to link it to another broad-gauge line, the Wilts, Somerset & Weymouth, which it was intended to join near Bruton. All of this suggests that it was destined to end up as a branch of the Great Western, linking two main lines in the same way that the Cheddar Valley route eventually did.

However, pushing up from the south coast of England came the Dorset Central Railway, and with it one of the great temptations of the 'Railway Age', a line linking the Bristol and English Channels and taking trade away from the sailing ships that had for centuries endured the delights of rounding the tip of Cornwall against the prevailing winds. And so it came to pass that the two 'Central' railways combined forces; the Somerset Central converted to standard gauge (at hefty expense) and instead of joining the WS&W at Bruton it crossed over it to where the two Central lines met at Cole. Thus was born the Somerset & Dorset Railway.

Unfortunately whilst the promoters had been thinking of the profits of their Channel to Channel route, steam ship design had been making progress and with the wind no longer such a hazard to navigation, the money did not flow in to the expected extent from a predominantly rural railway linking Highbridge with Poole via not too much along the way.

The next move was typically adventurous, or foolhardy (according to taste). The S&D promoted a line from Evercreech to Bath via the Somerset Coalfields in the Radstock area. This would link the Midland Railway at Bath to the South Coast and offer trade prospects from the North of England, but it also involved slogging over the Mendip Hills on ferocious gradients and along some sinuous sections of track. The line was complete by 1874, but by the time it was finished the S&D was bankrupt and in a bad way as regards engines and rolling stock. What happened next is a matter of skullduggery, chicanery and some controversy – in other words typical Victorian Railway politics.

Initially it looked like the Great Western would take over the bankrupt and disreputable S&D but whilst Paddington took its own sweet time, Derby was talking to Waterloo and the Somerset & Dorset Joint Railway came into being run by the Midland

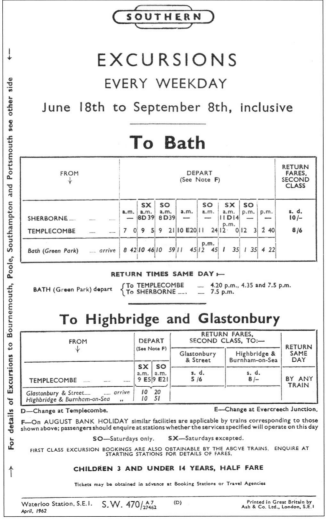

S&D Excursion Timetable for Summer 1962

and London & South Western Railways. The two big companies were very respectable and were in due course to make the SDJR a fine cross-country railway, but before they could get matters under control the old operational methods had led to a major and sanguinary head-on crash near Radstock. After that the reforms and improvements came steadily until the First World War.

The S&DJR came under the control of the London Midland & Scottish and Southern Railways after the 1923 grouping but then came steady atrophy. Schedules of trains remained virtually as per 1914 and some operational lunacies, like the arrangements at Templecombe where trains had to reverse direction on entering or leaving the station, with all the time that took, were never tackled as the bigger companies found more pressing demands elsewhere on their bank balances. Nor did nationalisation and British Railways bring any major changes.

Indeed it seemed that matters got worse. When more modern and powerful steam engines finally replaced 40-year-old machines in the mid-1950s, schedules remained as indolent as before, proving fatal as the private car and improvements in buses meant mounting competition. And passenger services were still planned as though they were competing companies rather than one supposedly co-ordinated whole. For example a look at connecting times for trains in this period suggests that anyone wishing to go from Glastonbury to Bristol was still expected to go via Evercreech Junction, Bath and Mangotsfield, rather than the more logical route with one change at Highbridge.

Nor were things greatly helped when the Western Region of B.R. took over the northern half of the line from the Southern Region which controlled the lot from 1948 to 1958. Looking at Western Region activity in the '50s and '60s it still clearly saw itself as the GWR and memories of the 1874 takeover were still harboured. Through traffic from the North of England to the South Coast began to go via Oxford and Basingstoke rather than Bath. This was probably partly through spite and also through operational considerations.

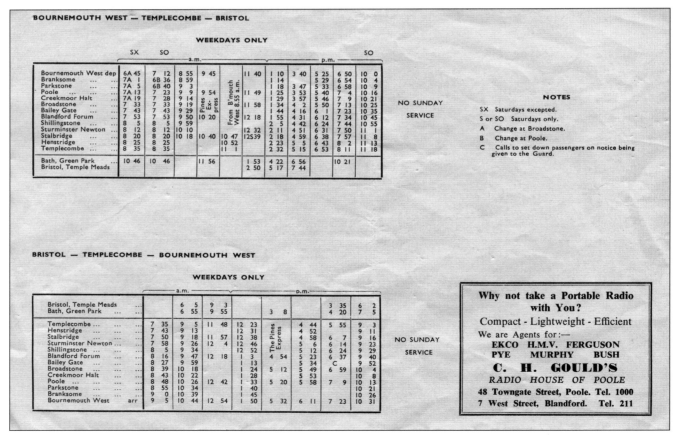

An extract from the Local Train Service timetable issued for the Bournemouth area covering the period from 2nd November 1959 to 12th June 1960. (*Author's collection*)

That pounding over the Mendips was still a major source of slower through speeds and higher operating costs and if there was spare capacity on the other lines it was sensible to use it. The holiday trains that had strained the S&D to its absolute capacity in the '50s disappeared in 1962, plus the line's flagship train, 'The Pines Express', which went to other routes. Even then timetables weren't changed and the remaining S&D trains ran to give 'connections' into long-distance trains that no longer ran. Closure was planned for 1965 but the last-minute withdrawal of one of the bus operators from the planned set of train replacements saw an 'emergency service' limp on until the start of March 1966. Some fragments remained after that for freight, gradually withering away until the last traces were gone from the railway map.

So what made the Somerset & Dorset so well loved that even the nickname 'Slow and Dirty' was delivered with some affection? The two counties through which it passed were and are very beautiful, with the contrasts of the Mendip Hills, the flatlands of the Somerset Levels through which the Highbridge line ran, the lush section of North Dorset and finally the seaside at Bournemouth with those pine trees. There were trains both local and bucolic ambling along and then through, long-distance trains or heavy freights. But most of all there was the staff. The S&D was a family railway. In many cases this was literally so, with generations working along the line, and in all cases figuratively so. The workforce knew each other and the people in the generally small communities it served, and that made for something very special that now seems other-worldly. Even in 1962-63 when the writing for the line was very clearly on the wall, the staff (including my Uncle Ted) strained long and hard, and risked their lives in appalling winter conditions over the Mendips to keep the trains moving and the towns and villages linked to the rest of Britain. It is that part of history that Alan Hammond's books have done so much to preserve for posterity.

BRITISH RAILWAYS
WESTERN AND SOUTHERN REGIONS

SOMERSET AND DORSET LINE

REVISION OF PASSENGER
TRAIN SERVICES
FROM

3rd JANUARY 1966
UNTIL FURTHER NOTICE

Owing to one of the road operators withdrawing his application for a licence to provide some of the alternative road services forming part of the consent conditions laid down by the Minister of Transport and the consequent postponement of the Licensing Court, it has become necessary to defer the date of closure of this line.

A new closing date has yet to be announced, but as from 3rd January, 1966, all existing passenger services between the following places will be suspended. An interim emergency service will be introduced, full details of which are contained in this pamphlet.

The sections of line concerned are:

Bristol (T.M.) to Bath Green Park

Bath Green Park to Bournemouth

Highbridge to Evercreech Junction

December 1965   Paddington and Waterloo

Printed by J. W. Arrowsmith Ltd., Bristol

(*left*) The front cover of the emergency timetable issued for the final two months of the S&D's existence. (*Author's collection*)

(*above*) The start of the Somerset & Dorset Railway at Bath Green Park station, with the very smart porteress, Joyce Ainsworth, c.1962. Looking at the train indicator finger boards, doesn't it bring it all back to you? If only the Swift and Delightful was still with us. (*Hugh Ballantyne*)

(*below*) The grounded body of a former Midland Railway sleeping car situated at Bath Green Park, which was once used for enginemen's Mutual Improvement classes and as a messroom, c.1935. (*Richard Dagger collection*)

(*right*) BR Standard class 4 No.75072 makes a spirited start collecting a three-coach set from the middle road at Bath Green Park. An unidentified Standard class 4 2-6-0 is ready to set off from the platform. (*John Pearce collection*)

(*below*) Bath Junction signalbox, with a telegraph pole, signals, lamp and steps purposely positioned to enable the signalman to attend easily to the single line tablet. In the sidings at the rear of the box there can be seen a SR open wagon with rounded ends. (*Keran A. Waldon collection*)

Steam activity at Bath Green Park in February 1965, with a class 8F No.48309 and a class 9400 0-6-0 Pannier Tank just behind. A lone shunter can just be seen on the right. It is the type of photograph in which you can smell the smoke and steam. *(Paul Strong)*

0-6-0PT No.3758 shunts empty coal wagons for the Radstock collieries at Bath Green Park in 1965. (*Paul Strong*)

(*above*) Happily smiling at the camera is driver Ray Stokes at Bath Green Park, with a Standard class Tank. He is lighting the headlamps in readiness for his return journey south. What a fine picture of an excellent railwayman. (*Alan Mitchard*)

(*above*) Wayne Mayo, fireman at Bath in the 1960s, looking out of the cab of a GWR 5700 class 0-6-0PT No.3681. Where has the number plate gone? Other footplate crews who worked out of Bath included: Ron Bean, Geoff Akers, Clive Cater, Howard Reynolds, Ian Bunnett, John Sawyer, Ivor Willshire, Ken Coffin, John Barber, Harry Starkey, Gustave Beeho, Eric Webber, Richard Kelson and Derek Coles. (*Wayne Mayo collection*)

(*below*) Driver Bert Reed (left) and fireman Wayne Mayo by the side of BR class 5 No.73001 at Bath Green Park. Look at the shine on Bert's shoes, and Wayne's winkle pickers remind me of what I used to wear in the 60s. (*Rita Smart collection*)

(*below*) A close up of a class 4, No.75073, at Bath Green Park with driver Vic Hunt (left) and his pal, station foreman Arthur Rowett. (*Keran A. Waldon collection*)

(*above*) Ted Smith, one of the senior drivers at Bath Green Park, looks out of the cab of Standard class 4 No.75073 in the 1960s. (*Alan Mitchard*)

(*above*) Fireman Bob Weaver (left) and driver Vic Hunt relax in the cab of class 4 No.75073 before taking out the 16.37 from Bath to Templecombe in the 1960s. (*Alan Mitchard*)

(*below*) Stanier LMS class 5 No.44964 which was based at Saltley when this photograph was taken in the 1950s. It is seen here at Bath locomotive depot with a group of passed cleaners; from left to right, Gordon Brickle, Robert (Geordie) Backhouse, Don Russell, my good friend the late Cliff Smith, Bob Wright and unknown. (*Alan Backhouse collection*)

(*below*) Mates together at Bath Green Park, 56 years ago. In front of a class 2, No.41242, are Roy Williams, Doug Farrent, Gordon Cross, Frank Eyles, Gordon Brickle, Gordon Scovell and in the front Ken Norris. (*Pat Bean collection*)

(*above*) Driver Reg Beasley, dressed in his railway uniform, is seen on his bike in Victoria Bridge Road, Bath. The photographer's NSU motorcycle leans against the railings. (*Alan Mitchard*)

(*above*) Arthur Rowett looks very pleased with himself, as he has his picture taken on an early model motorized platelayer's trolley. Mind you, there's not much protection from the weather. (*Keran A. Walden collection*)

(*below*) Looking up from the side of 9F No.92205 at the coal stage at Bath Green Park is Branksome driver Jim Tranter. Jim was a pigeon fancier and would often bring a basket of pigeons onto the footplate to release along the line. (*John Eaton*)

(*below*) Photographed at Bath Green Park in 1957 are fireman John Curtis (left) and driver Jack Thorne. They are standing in front of a Black 5 which they are getting ready for the down Pines Express. (*Ivo Peters, courtesy of Julian Peters*)

(*left*) Class 5, No. 73001, is caught in an idle moment at Bath Green Park shed. But who is having their photo taken and who is the photographer? (*Wayne Mayo collection*)

(*below*) GWR Castle class No.7023, *Penrice Castle* (85A Worcester shedplate), prepares to leave Bath Green Park northbound with the Home Counties Railway Society Special on 7th June 1964. This is believed to be the only appearance of a Castle locomotive at this station. (*Alan Mitchard*)

With the backdrop of 9F No.92220, *Evening Star*, at Bath Green Park, are, from left to right, station foreman Arthur Rowett, porter Fred Pitman and driver Fred Wotley. (*Keran A. Waldon collection*)

(*left*) Quite a rarity this, a Britannia Standard class, No.70033 *Charles Dickens*. The locomotive is at the head of a Pigeon Special in Bath Green Park goods yard, where the birds would be released. (*Alan Mitchard*)

1/9d to take your bicycle on a single journey was quite a sum when this ticket was issued in January 1931. (*Keith Barrett collection*)

(*below*) Sadly steam is coming to an end as a class 45 Peak diesel, No.D127, gets ready to leave Bath Green Park northbound. (*John Eaton*)

(*above*) Stanier class 8F No.48737 with the 08.15 Bath to Templecombe train runs through Lyncombe Vale towards Combe Down Tunnel. Note, on the left-hand side, that Devonshire Tunnel is obliterated with smoke and steam. (*Alan Mitchard*)

(*below*) A Stanier class 8F pilots an ailing 7F with a loaded coal train out of Combe Down Tunnel into Lyncombe Vale and down into Bath. The fireman on the 7F seems to be taking advantage of the welcome fresh air. (*Alan Mitchard*)

A scene at the northern end of the line on a beautiful spring day in 1954, as 2P No.40601 crosses Tucking Mill Viaduct with a passenger train bound for Templecombe. (*G.W. Sharp*)

Ken Stokes

It is often said that the railway is in your blood. That is certainly true of my family. My great grandfather, Charlie Stokes, was a coalman in 1890 at Bath Green Park and my grandfather, also called Charlie, was a driver on the S&D, as was my uncle Ray. My dad Ken was a booking clerk at Templecombe and my son Mark is a driver. For me at 15 years of age it was off to Swindon for a medical in 1961 with my mum. The minimum height was 5ft 4ins and I was just under that. They allowed me to start with the proviso that another medical was to be taken in six months time. In fact in those six months I grew another four inches.

In August of that year I started at Templecombe as a cleaner. I was referred to as a cabin boy, a title that would rattle my cage. However it wasn't a bad little number. Keeping the cabin, foreman's office, clerk's office and the signing-on lobby clean, allowed me to get to know everyone quite quickly. The downside to

the job was the toilet block – somebody had to keep it clean and that was me. With cider being the preferred tipple of some, and the strong laxative effect it had, the toilets had to be seen to be believed. Need I say more?

These duties took most of the morning; you might then go on to actually clean an engine. More often than not, though, cleaners at Templecombe in the early '60s could be found working on the coal stage, emptying ash pits, loading ash wagons, drain and tube cleaning or working in the sand house. On reflection it begs the question, what were the shed labourers doing?

One week after my 16th birthday I was sent to Bath for training to be passed out for firing. We were allowed two weeks for the programme, but being very keen I passed out in a week. I had a head start as Pat Evans ran the Mutual Improvement classes at Templecombe for firemen about to be passed for driving. He had no objection to me joining in with the likes of Robin Gould, Keith Barrett, Dave Young and Bill Trigg. There was a serious side to the class, but also a lot of good-natured banter; Thursday evening classes were quite entertaining.

Returning from Bath that week, Bill Gunning was the driver of the stopping passenger train that I had to catch. I got to know Bill from my cabin duties. Spotting me walking down the platform, he shouted out to me to come on to the footplate: 'You can stand behind me to see how it's done.' His mate fired as far as Midford, and then it was my turn. The engine, a Standard class 5, steamed well and I soon got to grips with the firing. The next day as I got onto the footplate with Bill, his mate picked up his bag, got off and went back down towards the coaches. Was it something I said? This was a bit much for me, as it was only day two and I might not get it right. Bill assured me we would be fine and anyway if it didn't go well he'd get his mate back. There was another problem; I'm right-handed and to fire Standards you had to be left-handed and Bill insisted I fired left-handed. Getting coal down to the front of the box didn't come easy. When I thought he wasn't looking I'd nip over to his side to fire with my right hand, but he was watching me like a hawk. His hat would come off and I would receive a hard clout, followed by some choice words. By the end of that week, after numerous whacks, I'd got the hang of it and felt confident about firing. In truth a Standard class 5 with three coaches and all stops is hardly a test for man and machine.

It would not be long before the real test came – 7th June 1962 and my first firing turn. It was the 2.10pm shift on station pilot duty with driver Alwyn Hannam on class 5700, No.3720. As a passed cleaner I kept a log of my firing turns, because as soon as 282 turns were completed you went on to first-year firing rate of pay, even if you were still a cleaner. Working with drivers, most of whom knew me as a schoolboy, was a pleasure. 21st June and only 32 firing turns under my belt, I'm booked with Lou Long on Standard class 4, No.75023 to assist the Pines Express. With nervous anticipation I prepare the loco, then it's light engine to Evercreech Junction. The Pines runs in headed by a 9F. We back on as the pilot, then right away; by Shepton Mallet all my nervousness has gone, 75023 is steaming well. The sound of two engines attacking the bank and working hard is awesome. It gives me a real buzz and I'm enjoying every minute.

At Bath it's onto the shed for coal and water ready for our return. For some reason the Branksome crew are given a West Country for the return run. After our break the Pines runs in from the north, we leave the shed and back onto the train. We leave on time and climbing away from Bath I can see Lou has the regulator open a bit more than on the up trip with the 9F. We come out of Devonshire Tunnel with 210lb of steam pressure, 10lb below the mark of 220. Now into Combe Down Tunnel, a short way in and to my surprise the valves lift. I open the firebox doors and the reflected light on our steam gauge still shows 210lb; it is the West Country blowing off steam. Then I hear the West Country start to slip. Lou lengthens the regulator of our engine 75023. I assume the WC driver closes his in order to regain control, and with that the noise from the West Country's safety valves rises even higher. The noise level is incredible, to be near any engine in the open when safety valves lift is unsettling. In the confines of a single-line narrow-bore tunnel, it is hell on earth. I'm not so much frightened, I'm terrified; at one stage I'm almost sitting on Lou's lap with my arm around him. It's impossible to speak to each other, the boiler exploding or the tunnel roof coming down runs through my mind. Eventually, after what seems like an eternity we come out of that tunnel; looking back I can see that the West Country was priming, little wonder the noise was so loud. She continues to blow for two or three more miles. Well, by now I'm in a bit of a state, my arms and legs have gone to jelly and I can't do a thing right and 75023 is beginning to suffer. Lou Long is a driver who knows the job backwards including mine. Not far south from Radstock and onto the bank he taps me on the shoulder and says, 'sit over my side, I'll give you a break' and this he does. It isn't long before 75023 is back on the mark. He continues to fire up the rest of the bank, and approaching the summit he says 'You're all right now, son' and comes back to the driver's side. With the remaining run down the bank to Evercreech, then light engine to Templecombe shed, the work has been done.

To work with drivers of Lou Long's calibre, I now appreciate, was a privilege. There were others, of course, like Walt Jeans, Den Norris, Ben Dyer, Jack Hix, Ray Stokes, Bert Jones, Derrick Howcutt and George Morley. Most drivers were a pleasure to work with, but there were a few that were not. They were hard going and difficult to communicate with.

One such driver, who I will not name, had a fearsome reputation for being a bit heavy with the regulator and rarely pulling the reverser back above 40% cut off. In the summer of 1963, now aged 17, I was booked to work an empty pigeon train back to Bath with this driver. Our engine was a 7F. I can't remember how many we had on, what I do recall is not seeing the end of the train when we pulled around the curve by Templecombe School.

Going down the bank past No.2 box the 7F is gathering speed; by Horsington Crossing my mate's got her really going like a long dog. A 7F at speed is a difficult footplate to be on, the cab rocks from side to side quite violently, as does the tender, and firing is an acquired art. In no time at all we approach Evercreech and the distant is on (sweet relief). Then we come to a stand at the North signalbox. Looking at my fire I realise there's a lot less than what I'd started with. My firing rate hasn't kept up with the demands of the boiler, so I quickly flash a couple of rounds into the box and then say to my mate: 'I'd better go and sign the book in the box, it looks like we might be here for a while'. 'No, you stay here, I'll do it', comes the reply and so muttering under his breath off he goes. Looking across to the yard there is no sign of the banker. I am quite convinced that with the weight of our train we are going to need it. The reason for our stopping is that a northbound freight has been let out in front of us taking the banker with it, so it's going to be a good half hour before it gets back. With this in mind I start to shovel more coal into the firebox, quite a lot more coal in fact; now let's see my mate hit that lot out. About five minutes later I'm pulling coal down in the tender and my mate climbs back onto the footplate, blows the whistle and the signal comes off. No, this can't be happening. I say: 'What about the banker?' and he replies 'I'm not waiting for that, I don't need him'. I reply: 'But look what I've done', as I show him the blacked-out fire. With a look of disgust he says: 'You'd better get the bar out', then promptly opens the regulator, and we are moving. I drive the bar deep into the firebox, yank down on it and my feet come off the floor, the bar doesn't move. I try again but not so deep, flames start to shoot through, a couple more jabs with the bar, then pull it around with the pricker, more flames appear. This is all taking too long though, a 7F boiler pressure is 180lbs, and ours is now down to 160. Evercreech New is passed; as yet the injectors haven't gone on, 160lb of steam,

half a glass of water, the regulator wide open, I'm in real trouble. At Prestleigh Viaduct the boiler pressure starts to rise to 170. On with the injector and off when pressure drops to 155, the bark from the 7F exhaust is somewhat muted. The distant is on for Shepton Mallet, and with the regulator eased, I get a chance to bring the water level up. As we near the end of the platform so the signal comes off, not enough time for a full recovery. So again the regulator handle is in the cab roof. The steam pressure never rises above 170, injectors on until pressure falls to 160, turn off again and so it goes on, the 7F steadily plodding up the bank with injectors never on long enough, the water level steadily falling. My mate doesn't enjoy the best of health, most of the time he is leaning out of his side of the cab and doesn't seem to be aware of our plight. As we come over the summit and level out, the water disappears out of the gauge glass. Now I put both injectors on, there is a real danger of dropping the lead plugs. The steam pressure with both injectors on falls quite quickly. My mate is still leaning out the side; boiler pressure falls to 100lb. The brakes go on and we grind to a halt; my mate looks at me somewhat surprised and says: 'We've stopped, turn those injectors off'. I shout back: 'We've got no water'. 'Turn them off' he insists; this I do under protest. By opening and closing the gauge glass drain cock quickly you can just make out the water bob up into the bottom nut. At 120lb of steam and no water showing the brakes come off. Over goes the regulator and away we go down the bank, 140lbs of steam, one injector back on and stays on. Eventually water starts to appear in the gauge glass. I can't remember how long we go with no water showing, it is too long for comfort. By Radstock steam pressure is back and the water level up. The remainder of the trip goes without incident. We return on the cushions without a word being spoken. I am glad to get home that night and put the whole episode down to experience.

My time on the Dorset was over before it began, just three years, but very enjoyable years. In 1964, I transferred to Gloucester, taking a well trodden path of ex-S&D men, like Frank Dyer, Tony Axford and Buzzy Hill who had gone the year before for promotion. Also at Gloucester there were various former drivers who worked on the S&D, Jim Heal, Howard Yeatman and Lou Long, who had two brothers, Percy and Jack working there also. The railway is in the blood of some families.

(*right*) A slightly misty view as 7F No.53807 passes Midford signalbox with a train for Bath. S&D guard Frank Staddon recalls on one occasion, the signalman, Percy Savage was in this box on a cold and misty night. Suddenly he could hear the rattling of chains and then the thud, thud of somebody walking up the veranda steps. Percy thought Old Nick was coming to get him. The door opened and an old man with a long white beard entered. To the relief of Percy, he only asked had he seen his goats as they had escaped from their enclosure. (*Roger Raisey*)

(*below*) 2P No.568 heads an unidentified Black 5 through Midford with a down express in 1950. (*R.K. Blencowe collection*)

(*above*) A scene to enjoy in 1965 as a Standard class 4 Tank No.80059 heads a three-coach train out of Midford towards Wellow. (*E.T. Gill/R.K. Blencowe collection*)

(*below*) A classic shot on the viaduct at Midford as 4MT No.75072 makes its way south with the 16.35 train from Bath to Templecombe. (*R.E. Toop*)

The last public service day was Saturday 5th March 1966. Here BR class 4 No.80043 driven by Cecil Waldron and fired by Wayne Mayo, leaves Wellow with the 4.25pm Bath Green Park to Templecombe train. This was the last train to leave Bath in daylight and the penultimate departure. *(Hugh Ballantyne)*

(*above*) 4F No.44146 pilots a West Country class No.34108, *Wincanton*, near Wellow on 27 July 1957. (*E.W. Fry/R.K. Blencowe collection*)

(*right*) Driver Bill Gunning in the cab of a 7F on a holiday special. Bill came from a long line of family members who worked on the S&D which included his brothers Archie and Tom. (*Ken Stokes collection*)

(*below*) Large boiler 7F No.13808 drifts around a curve near Wellow. Interesting to note the year is 1936 and apart from the bogie wagon with the load of timber, all the other wagons are of wooden construction. (*H.C. Casserley*)

(*above*) Class 2P No.40634 pilots Standard class 5 No.73047 near Shoscombe in June 1957. (*E.W. Fry/R.K. Blencowe collection*)

(*below*) Class 7F No.53809 runs through Radstock station with a short mixed freight heading towards Bath. On the road alongside is a Co-op mobile shop. (*Alan Mitchard*)

Ron Hatcher

I started on the railway as a cleaner at Templecombe Motive Power Department in 1947; I was 17 years old. In addition to cleaning the engines, we were often put on to the tube rodding, emptying ash pits, assisting in firebox repairs and the coaling of engines. During my time as a cleaner I got to know many of the staff; people such as John Caesar, Wilf Jeans, Maurice Miles, Charlie Watkins and Stan Morey come to mind amongst many others.

Eventually the day came when I was told to go out on the footplate to learn how to fire an engine. The driver was Jack Loader, while the fireman was Dennis Nettley, the engine a class 7F. I did my best, but by the time I'd had a go at firing there was coal all over the footplate; I managed to throw it everywhere except into the firebox. I still remember Jack saying he was going to have a word with the workshop to see if the hole could be made bigger. Even though I didn't cover myself in glory the first time out, I soon became a passed cleaner and covered for passed firemen on rest days and sickness.

Shortly after I started, I got a call at home to tell me to book on at nine that evening, to fire the night train to Poole. I duly went in and signed on. I was to be firing for driver Bert Jones. When Bert saw me he assumed that I was there to assist and learn from an experienced fireman. He said: 'My mate's late tonight, we'll be late off shed if he doesn't get here soon'. I told him: 'I'm your mate tonight, Bert'. He looked at me, still only 17 remember, and asked if I had ever fired a class 7 on my own. When I told him I hadn't, Bert really lost his temper. The Poole run was a tough one for a fireman; the engine would be pulling 55 wagons fully laden with clay. It was quite a tall order for a boy to keep the engine well enough fired to haul that lot. Bert said be wasn't going to take me as his fireman and stormed off to see Doug Barnard, the night chargeman. By all accounts Doug told him: 'I'm not changing it, I've got no-one else and you've got to take him'. Bert had to give in and take me along, but as you can imagine, he didn't start the trip as a very happy man. However, we had a beautiful trip down, and coming back with a full load on I managed to surpass Bert's gloomy expectations and keep full steam. All was well with Bert's world now, and he was as happy as a sandboy all the way back. We got back into Templecombe at about 03.30.

I was weary, but very happy too. Bert was always nice to me after that trip, and that engine, No.53810, was ever after a favourite of mine.

One night, sometime in 1948, I was firing to Leo Elkins; we were taking an ammunition train to Bath using engine 7F No.53809. We had a banked load from Evercreech Junction and had a good trip up to Binegar. The banker came off, and on we went to Midford where we picked up the single-line tablet and opened her up to get through the tunnel. Unfortunately the engine started priming and we gradually lost power, finally coming to a complete halt just inside Combe Down Tunnel. As we backed out I glanced back down the train towards the lights of the guard's van. I could see them accelerating away from me! A coupling had broken and the back half of the train had consequently broken away, and was off back down the line to Midford. This caused us a bit of consternation. We got to a phone as fast as possible to let the Midford signalman know about their unexpected arrival and to get permission to go back and re-couple. We then backed down to the bottom of the dip near Midford station and re-coupled the rear half, but we now had another problem. The train was just too heavy for us to move from a standing start up out of the dip. We had to ring Bath to get another engine out to help us. After a good wait, 53808 came out and got us into Bath. We left the train in the yard, turned the engine and went back light engine. Once the shift finished I set off for home in the pouring rain thinking what an eventful night it had been. Little did I know that there was more to come.

When I got home I put my mac into the cupboard and began to wash up and get ready for bed. Then I became aware that I could smell smoke. I wandered round the house, eventually tracing it back to the cupboard. I opened the cupboard door to find that my mac was smouldering. I grabbed it and threw it outside into the rain. As it hit the fresh air the coat burst into flames. It didn't look too special, once the rain had put the blaze out. I thought about what might have happened if I hadn't smelt the smoke. I then tried to work out what had caused a perfectly ordinary, guaranteed non-self-combusting mac to burst into flames. It couldn't have been a cinder; my mac had been in a locker at the time. I hadn't had time or the opportunity to smoke a cigarette myself. I suspected that one of the lads at work had dropped a cigarette butt into my pocket for a joke. The next night at work I tried to find out if anyone knew what had happened. Everyone there thought the whole thing hilarious and no-one was going to admit to anything. To this day I don't know how the fire came home with the fireman.

Saturday mornings in the summer were always very busy. Special trains were leaving Bournemouth every 15 to 20 minutes packed with holidaymakers returning to the Midlands. Templecombe used to send down spare sets of men to help cover the demand for staff to run these trains. One Saturday I was sent down to fire for Donald Beale. Donald was a real gentleman, a fine engineman, and a lovely man to fire to. That morning we came out of Bournemouth West with 11 coaches behind an Ivatt class 4 engine, the type we used to know as the Doodlebug. They were unreliable engines with a reputation for poor steaming. We had a reasonable trip to Evercreech Junction and when we got there a class 2P engine joined on the front to assist us. We then set off over the Mendips. True to Doodlebug form, when Donald opened the regulator fully, the steam gauge dropped, she didn't like the heavy working. I had to let the water go just to try to keep the pressure up. By the time we pulled up at our scheduled stop at Shepton Mallet the water was getting rather low. I asked Donald if he was going to wait there a while to get a bit of water back and raise a bit more steam pressure. I knew that had I been the driver I would have done so. Not Donald. 'We'll carry on, we'll be all right', he said.

We kicked off from Shepton Mallet and signalled to the assisting engine that we were down the pan. Her driver opened her right up to help us out, while I shovelled coal like a madman; I put the bar in; I put

Sentinel 0-4-0T No.47191 and by her side 0-6-0T No.47465 taken from inside Radstock engine shed. Wally Moon, a stalwart of Radstock shed for many years, fired and drove these engines along with Eric Wilson, Aubrey Pearce, Dennis Curtis, Bert Ashley, Horace Clark, Desmond Kemp (known as Jack), Frank Kemp, Dennis Love, Bert Webster and many more. (*Wally Moon collection*)

the pricker in, I did everything I knew to try to get steam up, but to no avail. Donald meanwhile sat there looking serene. You would have thought from his demeanour that we had a full head of steam. He was completely confident that all would be well. We turned the top at Masbury Summit with 120lb of steam (ideally it should have been 225lb) and the water bobbing in the nut. As we hit the down slope we got both injectors going. The water then totally disappeared from the glass. I was convinced we were about to drop a plug; Donald was still completely unconcerned. We got down the bank to Radstock where the track levelled out again. I saw that we had about an inch of water in the glass. As you would expect with both injectors going, we hadn't made a pound of steam on the down slope, and so we travelled from Radstock to Bath with the regulator barely open. The 2P was doing most of the work, as we pulled in at Bath station with about 100lb of steam and a quarter of a glass of water. It was without doubt the worst trip I ever had in all my years on the railway. It left me with great respect for Donald though; he recognized the limitations of that engine and he knew exactly how far he could push it without disaster striking it. I had been rather depressed by the trip, but Donald was still happy enough. He thought we had done all we could with that engine on that run. 'You did your best and I suppose you can't ask more than that', he said.

Eventually I became a registered fireman and I went into the passenger link, usually firing to driver Charlie Stokes. I got on well with Charlie; I used to oil the big ends for him when we were preparing an engine, and he used to rake out the ash pan when we were disposing of one. I remember a particularly bad trip we had together one time. We relieved the Templecombe men at No.2 box on the 11.40 from Bournemouth. The engine was a 4F and the assisting engine came on at Evercreech Junction. When we arrived at Bath we went to the loco shed where we were told by the shed foreman that there had been an engine failure and our engine would be required to work another turn. So we had to hang about and wait for another engine to come in. Eventually a West Country class came in; we were told it had been out all day and had a dirty firebox. As departure time was getting very close, there was only time to take on coal and water before going off shed. I had no time to do anything to the fire, but I managed to liven up what was in the box with the aid of the bar and the pricker. By the time our train came in we had quite a reasonable fire going. We were taking on nine coaches with no assisting engine available (nine was overloaded for a single engine), so given the state of the fire I wasn't looking forward to going up over the Mendips.

We pulled away from Bath station and got up through the tunnels all right. Charlie nursed the train to Radstock. Then we got into the bank with the regulator wide open and that's where the trouble started. I was prepared for it though; I had the dart and the pricker on the footplate with me. In addition to firing, I was using both fire irons to liven up the fire as much as possible. We struggled on up the bank clearing the top with steam pressure down at 140lbs, the water nearly down in the nut, but an amazing 21 inches of vacuum. As we went down the bank to Evercreech Junction I got a bit more life into the fire and the water level well up, then we coasted to Templecombe where a new crew relieved us. It was the end of a very eventful day. A couple of days later I saw our relief crew, they too had had a bad time of it. They had struggled all the way down to Bournemouth and by the time they pulled into the shed they had a box that was full of nothing but clinker.

In 1958 I was going for my driving exam; I went up to Bath and met the inspector on the station. For my test I had to drive a stopping train down to Evercreech Junction where we got off. We walked up to the sidings and picked up a freight train which I had to drive down to Glastonbury. There I changed over with a Highbridge man who had brought a freight train up from his home station and worked back to Evercreech Junction, from where we went passenger back to Bath. On the way up to Bath there were questions from the rule book and on the engine. Once we got to Bath the inspector bought the tea and cakes at the buffet and then grilled me with a few more questions. At the end of it all, came the good news that I had passed. Unfortunately I didn't get much longer to work on the railways. My time with the S&D came to a close in 1959 when hearing problems meant I had to reluctantly give it all up.

Every man at Templecombe depot I regarded as a mate. It was a pleasure to have worked with them all. To this day I still have a mint of memories about the days of steam and the wonderful characters who worked on the S&D.

(*left*) Shunting work completed and ready to bank the coal train to Masbury Summit. In front of the ageing 3F No.47276 are, from left to right, shunter Lawrence (Larry) Dando, driver Wally Moon and fireman Eric Wilson. Wally was a passed fireman who always wore a tie when he was on driving duties. (*Wally Moon collection*)

(*below*) 3F No. 47557 with driver Aubrey Pearce keeping his hand in as a fireman on a banking turn, c.1958. (*Wally Moon collection*)

(*above*) A busy scene in the distance as an unidentified 3F is seen at Norton Hill Colliery hauling 17 trucks of coal and a guard's van. (*Frank Kemp collection*)

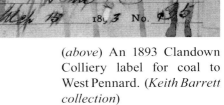

(*above*) An 1893 Clandown Colliery label for coal to West Pennard. (*Keith Barrett collection*)

(*left*) An unusual pairing on the S&D is T9 No.30120 piloting West Country class No.34043, *Combe Martin*. This photograph was taken between Midsomer Norton and Radstock in mid July 1957. (*Author's collection*)

Coming into Midsomer Norton is Standard class 5 No.73054 with the 09.53 Bath to Bournemouth service. In the right background can be seen Norton Hill Colliery. This station is now the site of the Somerset & Dorset Railway Heritage Trust. They are doing a superb job and the station is well worth a visit. (*Alan Mitchard*)

Running through Midsomer Norton in 1960 is Standard class 4 No.75023 assisting an unidentified Standard class 5 with a down express. (*Keith Barrett collection*)

(*above*) A stunning photograph of Midsomer Norton station gardens taken in the 1930s. If only it was in colour. (*Norman Cray collection*)

(*right*) The photographer is taking his life in his hands by taking this photo on the up starting signal at Midsomer Norton, c.1930s. Only the gentleman on the right looks familiar, believed to be stationmaster Frank Franks. Who are the other three people? (*Norman Cray collection*)

(*left*) Driver Lou Long with fireman Alan Hix on the footplate of class 5 No.73047. This class of loco was introduced in 1951 and designed at Doncaster. (*Alan Mitchard*)

(*below*) Bath driver, Dick Evry, turns to make a joke to his fireman Cliff Smith (out of view) who is taking a drink of cold tea whilst working 73054 between Midsomer Norton and Chilcompton on the 9.53 Bath Green Park to Bournemouth West train, on the 13th August 1961. (*Hugh Ballantyne*)

(*left*) Standard class 5 No.73054 restarts its train away from Midsomer Norton and heads for Bournemouth. In the yard an unidentified Jinty waits for the line to clear. (*Alan Mitchard*)

(*below*) Having worked the 12.35pm freight from Bath to Norton Hill Colliery with 7F No.53809, the fireman, Mike Ryall, now changes the lamps at Midsomer Norton station, before running round and heading another freight train back to Bath. (*Alan Mitchard*)

(*above*) A stirring action shot of 4F No.44422 (now preserved) piloting a fellow 4F No.44558, as they leave Chilcompton Tunnel on 6 September 1954. (*E.W. Fry/R.K. Blencowe collection*)

(*below*) A splendid view in July 1961 of 9F No.92001 making its way through Chilcompton station with a Bournemouth to Bradford train. (*E.W. Fry/R.K. Blencowe collection*)

(*above*) Chilcompton signalbox captured in warm sunlight. The box had 13 levers and no shunting signals, which is unusual. Note the water column on the right and how neat and tidy everything looks. (*David Strawbridge collection*)

(*below*) Class 2P No.40564 heads an unidentified Stanier Black 5 with a train at Burnt House Bridge No.57 near Moorewood. (*David Strawbridge collection*)

Robin Gould

I left school around Christmas 1953. When leaving school you hoped to get an apprenticeship either in the building industry or engineering. The railways and farming were also avenues of employment. To get on the railway, it helped to have family or friends working there. The railway was a job for life, and to get into the motive power department was the icing on the cake. Some lads had to start in the traffic department or the station yard and then transfer back to the loco shed which meant losing seniority. I was lucky when I had a job interview with the shedmaster at Templecombe loco, Mr. Butler, who used to travel from Bournemouth on the first up train in the morning. At my interview I was told only to speak when asked to. Mr. Butler told me all about driver Charlie Gould, who was a senior driver with over 40 years' service. If I was thinking of joining the loco depot, he was looking for the same example from me. Mr. Butler never once asked if I was a relation to Charlie. In fact we are not related – mind you I used to be his paperboy. So with the excellent record of Charlie ringing in my ears I then went for a medical at Eastleigh.

Templecombe loco was then under the Southern Region. On passing my medical I started on 18th January 1954 as an engine cleaner. In fact, I did not clean many engines because I was only 15 and could not work nights. I worked early and late turn for the first 12 months. On early turn the first job in winter was to clean out and re-light the two fires in Jim Fry's (roster clerk) room and Mr. Butler's office, then scrub the two floors. The floor covering was thick brown hessian-backed lino. After a while it would go from brown to off-white. If Mr. Butler came in and saw a dark shadow (caused by men walking in and out all day with oil, grease and coal dust) I had to do it again. After office duty it was up the station for the mail and odd spare engine parts. Some were sent down from Bath for LMS engines and some from Bournemouth for the SR engines. In winter you checked all fire devils and made up fires at the water columns. Then it was back to the loco and report to the shed engineman Charlie Guy; he would move engines about the shed and I would pull the points and take the tender brakes off for him. I would also help the steamraisers, Walt Webb or Ern Cawley, by getting the old wagon boards to light up the engines. Also I helped Joe Dyer the boilersmith with the arch bricks for the fire boxes. The

highlight of the day after Jim Fry had done the rosters for the next day, was taking call notes to drivers and firemen in Templecombe and surrounding villages. At that time Doug Barnard and Jack Loader were the late and night chargemen. The senior passed cleaner was Dennis Randall; his father Bill was a goods guard. At 16 you passed out for firing duties on a day-to-day basis; it was only on the summer timetable that you would be booked out every day. I was fortunate at Templecombe that we not only covered our own work, but also at Salisbury, Bournemouth Central, Branksome, Evercreech Junction, Highbridge, Radstock and Bath.

Salisbury men would go to Nine Elms, London because of a shortage there; Yeovil and Templecombe passed cleaners would go to Salisbury. Our main job was preparation and disposal of engines on shed and shovelling coal forward on the down Waterloo and up Exeter expresses at the station. It was always very interesting working with the Evercreech men like Donald Webb, Cecil Cooper, Clarence Rawles and Derek (Tanker) Jones. They had three turns, early turn was 06.05. On one early turn with Donald Webb we were approaching Elbow Corner Crossing, trying to find the signal in the dark which protected the gates. Donald shouted across to me: 'It's just like the Grand National, 15 hurdles between Evercreech Junction and Highbridge'. What he was telling me was that there were many crossing gates, some with and some without signals. Roy Miles, one of our guards, had a brother Eric who with his wife Joyce were crossing keepers at Cemetery Lane; later Eric went on to be a signalman.

On the afternoon turn you would shunt the yards around the stations. While working with Donald on this turn we arrived at Evercreech New station. I realized I had forgotten my wife's birthday card. I asked Donald if I could pop up to the village to get one, little did I know how far it was. Donald said: 'All right, I'll wait outside the goods shed for you to come back.' When I got back there was no Donald or engine. I asked the signalman what had happened and he said that the engine was needed back at Evercreech Junction. He had taken the porter off the station to fire to him. I had to follow down on the next train.

I remember a Templecombe loco man on the Shillingstone goods. It was market day and he had bought some live ducks. On arriving back at the station he now had to decide where to put them. After much deliberation it was decided to put them in the tender of the engine where they could swim around freely. All the shunting after this was done very carefully, so as not to cause waves in the tender. All went well until they arrived back on shed at Templecombe; the water in the tender by now had gone down. The only way to get them out was by filling the tender water tank, but great care had to be taken while doing this. If the water pressure was turned on too fast it would drown the ducks. So as the water rose the ducks were rescued. After this, if you were looking for the water level in the boiler on this engine and you could see a duck in the gauge glass, you had water in the boiler!

On the night turn you would shunt yards and bank trains to Binegar. If you were lucky you might get to *The Pecking Mill* pub for supper, with Sheila Ashman on piano; her brother was a signalman at the Junction station box.

After about five years I was made up to a fireman. You started off in the top end yard at Templecombe shunting the goods trains, such as the Shillingstone and Blandford goods. One of the drivers I worked with was Art Hatcher. I then went into the main goods link with George Eason, a former Yeovil Town driver. All the Yeovil Town men were good, especially on summer Saturdays coming out of Bath with the West Country classes; mind you they were prone to slipping. You had to be set up before going into the tunnels at Bath. If you were slipping on entering you knew you were in for a rough trip, sulphur fumes, smoke and heat. Although the tunnel at Devonshire was short you were still climbing up the bank; if you were lucky you would be down to walking pace. There were times when if you were slipping badly the only way to know you were going forward was to put your fingers on the tunnel wall; if they bent back you were still going forward.

The Black 5s, 7Fs and all the Standard classes were by far the best for the S&D. It was a pity the Standard 9Fs had not come sooner; they would have saved a lot of hard work and bad language. For the last six years and up to closure of the line I fired to Dennis Norris in the passenger link. Dennis was a great character; a Justice of the Peace, N.U.R. Union Secretary, on the Loco Department Committee, Chairman of the Village Council and a member of the Wells Labour party constituency, through which he fought very hard against the closure. I am pleased he lived long enough to see Templecombe station open again. During the six years with Dennis we had quite a few bad trips.

I am sure without Dennis's skill as an engineman we would have stopped for a blow up on many occasions.

One of the Templecombe turns was the 12.00 to Bath returning with the 16.21 Bath to Bournemouth train. We normally had a Southern Standard 4 class Nos.76025-27 from Bournemouth Central shed. Generally they were good steamers, but not on this turn. The engines were always in a poor state, such as dirty tube plates, leaking tubes and poor coal. Worst of the bunch was 76026; she would not steam with a high or low fire. We would struggle getting to Bath, some days you could clean the fire at Bath, take on fresh coal and leave the station with a full head of steam. On coming out of Combe Down Tunnel towards Midford you would be coasting to give up the single-line tablet. The steam gauge would read 160lbs of pressure and half a glass of water if you were lucky. At Radstock we would be in the same state for the climb up to Masbury Summit. Dennis had a great sense of humour and would say: 'Are you putting the coal in upside down'. If you were going to stop for a blow up you would always try to make Binegar. It was very rare to stop for a blow up because the crews felt they had failed if they stopped for steam. It was better to lose a minute or two going up hill and make it up going down the other side. There have been many occasions when we have been looking for the water to appear in the gauge glass after coming over Masbury Summit.

On another trip, Dennis and I were working the 17.30 Bournemouth West to Templecombe with 41243. We had no problems going down to Bournemouth with the 12.23, but on leaving Bournemouth West station there was no blast or draw on the fire with the regulator open. We were in a sorry state on arriving at Branksome. After coasting down the hill to Poole we then decided to try and make Blandford where there was an up goods from Poole which was always referred to as the 76 up goods. We got as far as Sturminster Newton about 20 minutes late. We were assisted by the 76 up goods engine to Templecombe. On opening the smokebox door at Templecombe loco it was found that all the self-cleaning sieves had fallen onto the blast pipe, cutting off the blast to the chimney.

On closure I moved to Westbury loco, and became a driver in 1973. I stayed to retirement, completing 50 years all but six weeks. I have no doubt that the first 12 years' experience on the S&D and the assistance from all grades helped me to complete the last 38 years. As I was told on joining in 1954, it was a job for life.

So. West. and Mid. Railway Companies'
Som. and Dor. Joint Line. (827)

TO PAY PARCEL.

FROM BINEGAR

To

WEIGHT OF CONSIGNMENT. Lbs.	PARTICULARS.	AMOUNT £ s. d.		
	Paid on			
	Collection			
NUMBER OF PACKAGES.	**Carriage,** C.R.			
	,, O.R.			
	TOTAL TO PAY			

(*above*) A majestic sight at Binegar of 2P No.40509 piloting WC class No.34044, *Woolacombe*, with this express from Bournemouth to Sheffield. (*Keith Barrett collection*)

(*below*) 7F 2-8-0 No.53807 (22C) runs past Binegar at the head of a down goods train. A Jinty Tank can be seen banking in the rear, which will only go to the top of Masbury Summit then return light engine. (*Keith Barrett collection*)

(*right*) On 2 March 1958 driver George Welch enjoys a break in the cab of 7F No.53804, after ballast working at Binegar. (*George Welch collection*)

(*below*) An extract from the 1902 summer timetable.

SATURDAY AFTERNOON EXCURSIONS
TO THE
Mendip Hills,
CHILCOMPTON (for DOWNSIDE ABBEY),
MASBURY (for WELLS CATHEDRAL,) &c.
EVERY SATURDAY during JULY, AUGUST & SEPTEMBER,
A Cheap Excursion Train will leave BATH (Mid. station) at 1.30 p.m. for

STATIONS.	RETURN FARE. Third Class.	STATIONS.	RETURN FARE. Third Class.
RADSTOCK Midsomer Norton and Welton Chilcompton	1s. 3d.	SHEPTON MALLET Evercreech New	1s. 9d.
Binegar Masbury	1s. 6d.	Evercreech Junction	

The SCENERY OF THE MENDIPS is remarkably Picturesque. WELLS, with its MAGNIFICENT CATHEDRAL, is Three miles only from Masbury Station, and the Road between the two points commands extensive and varied Views of the surrounding country.
THESE TICKETS will be available for return by any ORDINARY TRAIN on date of issue only.

(*left*) It looks cramped in the cab of class 5 No.73047. The crew on this engine were working on a BR Emergency Single Line Working film in October 1956. On the footplate, from left to right, are driver Art Hatcher, pilotman Jim Gould and fireman Cliff Day. (*SDRT collection*)

A joy to see as 4F No.44417 sweeps around the curve at Masbury in April 1954. It looks like the track gang has been busy with the fresh amount of ballast on the trackbed. (*E.W. Fry/R.K. Blencowe collection*)

Working hard at Masbury, with plenty of smoke and steam on view, is 3F No.43593 piloting West Country No.34102, *Lapford*. (*E.W. Fry/R.K. Blencowe collection*)

(*above*) Having just banked a down freight train to the top of Masbury Summit, Jinty 0-6-0T No.47496 returns bunker first to Binegar, wrong road, on 17th June 1957. Note the Masbury down distant signal in the off position. (*E.W. Fry/R.K. Blencowe collection*)

(*below*) A splendid shot in August 1953 at Masbury Summit. In harness are 4F No.44102 and class 5 No.44826 with a passenger train. (*E.W. Fry/R.K. Blencowe collection*)

(*above*) Almost at the top of Masbury Summit is class 2P No.40697 and an unidentified Standard class 5 with the (555) 8.20am (SO) Bristol to Bournemouth express. It's just passed under bridge No.69 Oakhill Road Bridge and will soon descend towards Evercreech Junction. (*Keith Barrett collection*)

(*below*) Running at speed near Shepton Mallet is 2P No.40696 and Standard class 5 No.73050 with the (M223) 9.03am Birmingham to Bournemouth train in August 1959. (*Keith Barrett collection*)

(*above*) An express powered by 2P 4-4-0 No.40634 and an unidentified Black 5 drifts down through Shepton Mallet. (*Keith Barrett collection*)

(*below*) Maxwell Shore had obviously impressed his stationmaster. I wonder what he made of his RAF career. (*Max Shore collection*)

E.R.O. 9

LONDON MIDLAND AND SCOTTISH RAILWAY COMPANY

Telephone:

YOUR REFERENCE ....

OUR REFERENCE

SHEPTON MALLET

DEPARTMENT

STATION

14. 6. 47

Maxwell Shore has been employed by the LM & S Rly at Shepton Mallet since 1943 as junior porter. He has proved satisfactory, always obedient, honest, & trustworthy ~ He is a good sportsman & organiser, and an active member of the local O.T.C. With good supervision he should make a good airman and citizen.

G F Coles   Station Master

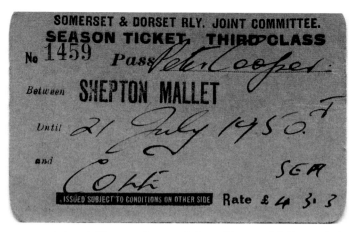

(*above*) Two well-known S&D characters. Guard Roy Miles (left) and foreman at Evercreech Junction Vic Freak, are enjoying a day out at the Royal Bath and West showground, Shepton Mallet. (*Vic Freak collection*)

(*above*) Six months travel from Shepton Mallet to Cole for £4.3s.3d? Quite a difference to today's prices but it was over half a century ago. (*Keith Barrett collection*)

(*below*) A view of the station as BR Standard class 2-6-4T No.80081 runs into Shepton Mallet Charlton Road with the 9.05 Templecombe to Bath Green Park train in 1965. (*Paul Strong*)

John Eaton

I started on the Somerset & Dorset Railway at Evercreech New, after leaving the Army in August 1954. For a short period of time I gained experience about the workings of the station; I then went into the station's signalbox as a temporary trainee signalman. One day during my training with signalman Sid Pitt, I had taken on the 11.00am mixed freight from Bath to Evercreech Junction. As it was passing our signalbox, I accidentally reversed the signal too early. The freight train stopped in section about ¼ mile from the signal. The driver walked back from the engine to enquire what was wrong. In the end I had a caution from the stationmaster Reg Jeans and the signalman Sid Pitt had a caution from the District Inspector Mr. Elliott. After three months, the temporary post of signalman was discontinued, so I had to go back as a porter at Evercreech New.

After a while I was moved onto the Western Region before I returned to porter's duty at Evercreech Junction. On one occasion, whilst on late turn at Evercreech Junction, I was getting parcels and mail out of the last up passenger train, which was the 9.15pm transfer to the 9.25pm Evercreech Junction to Highbridge. I had the parcel trolley fully loaded with mail and parcels. I was backing the trolley on a slight slope near a large Fox Bush hedge. Somehow I slipped and landed in the hedge on my back, with my feet in the air and the trolley handle between my legs – a rare sight to be had and very, very painful. As I screamed for help, the station foreman came over and started to laugh as did the nearby passengers. The parcel trolley was removed and the parcels put on the last branch passenger train. The hedge now had a very large hole. When I came on duty the next day the stationmaster and platform staff asked me what had happened. When I told them,

Relaxing on the steps of the signalbox is Evercreech New signalman Sid Pitt, c.1950s. Note the lime kiln in the background. (*George Gillard collection*)

they all had a jolly good laugh at my expense. I was not amused as it had hurt my pride.

Some years later I got the signal lampman post at Evercreech Junction. I always attended the signal lamps at the station on Mondays. On one particular Monday it was raining very heavily with storms and strong winds. I always left the very tall signal lamp until last. I had the new signal lamp strapped in the holder to my waist, to allow me to go up the ladder and have my hands free to climb. I had climbed up the signal and taken the old signal lamp out and put it on the signal platform. A strong gust of wind blew the old signal lamp off the signal platform and onto the railway line; it exploded with a loud bang. On duty in Evercreech South signalbox was relief signalman Sid Ashman, who looked out of the window and said with a laugh: 'Now, John, you will be in big trouble'. I replied: 'I know I am'. After descending from the signal I went into the stationmaster's office which was on the opposite platform (down) next to the double arm signal and told Alec Stowe what had occurred and what signalman Sid Ashman had said. Mr. Stowe had a laugh and all was forgotten. The signal lamp was sent to the signal and telegraph department at Frome to be repaired.

When I was a porter I remember a summer Saturday, when the 4.21pm from Bath to Bournemouth West came into Evercreech Junction. On arriving at the station the guard saw some smoke coming out of a coach axle box (hot box). He reported this to me and went back to examine the axle box. I informed the station foreman Mark Lambert, who told the stationmaster Mr. Stowe. He went to Evercreech North to fetch the Junction shunting engine, to come to the rear of the train. I assisted in detaching the coach and the front coaches were drawn forward to clear. I undid the vacuum pipe of the front portion to keep the train from moving. The Junction engine took the rear part up the middle siding and the disabled coach was put into the station sidings. After more shunting to get everything in the right position, I felt quite proud of what I had achieved. The Bournemouth guard wondered why the porter could do the shunting. Mark Lambert said: 'He knows how to shunt coaches as he was a passenger shunter at Westbury'. Mr. Stowe and Mark thanked me very much for assisting them. After a quick wash I had a well-earned pint next door at the *Railway Hotel*. On the Monday the carriage was examined and temporarily repaired. It was sent back to Bristol; the coach had an old North Eastern coach buck-eye connection.

I remember driver John Dray telling me about signalman Reg Padfield when he was relieving at Evercreech South signalbox. He saw the Evercreech Junction shunter arrive to take water. Reg looked out of the window and saw Derek (Tanker) Jones at the water column. He said: 'Tanker, what's that horse show up at Binegar called, where horses jump?' Derek replied: 'I don't know what you mean'. Reg answered: 'Gymnackerams, you know'. Derek was con-fused; after some thought he said to Reg: 'You mean gymkhana' to which Reg replied: 'That's what I said'.

There was another time when I had just finished my duty at the Junction on a Saturday night. I was waiting to see my friend, driver John Dray. He was coming back from Bath with the assisting engine on a returning football special from Manchester to Bournemouth; the football match was an F.A. cup tie. On arrival at Evercreech the assisting engine was detached whilst the train engine took on water for the journey south. John Dray went to the signalbox to ask the signalman on duty, who was Les Williams, if he could go over to the pub with his fireman to have some liquid refreshment. Les replied: 'Carry on, my dear, you have your pints and I'll be over soon'. After the train had gone Les came over to have his refreshment. John was a little worried and said to Les: 'I think we should go'. Les replied: 'When I say we should go, then we go'. He continued drinking his pint. Some time later John worked his light engine back to Templecombe.

On another occasion at the Junction, passenger guard Roy Miles had seen stationmaster Jack Pike leave his hand lamp outside the porter's cabin at Evercreech Junction. When Jack went into the booking office Roy put a sprat into his hand lamp. Jack wondered why he always had the smell of fish cooking when he lit his lamp.

Porter George Gillard who worked on the S&D for over ten years, c.1950s. In the background is Evercreech New signalbox. (*George Gillard collection*)

I recall the first Pines Express to travel on the S&D from Bournemouth West to Bath Green Park without an assisting engine. The Western Region tried several ways to do away with the assisting engines from Evercreech Junction to Bath. They controlled the line from Cole to Bath and on to Mangotsfield, Gloucester and beyond. They decided to introduce the 9Fs to take the 9.45am Bournemouth West to Manchester Pines Express un-assisted from the Junction. On this particular day the Pines Express was worked with a 9F with driver Donald Beale, fireman Peter Smith and guard Leonard Rossiter. On arrival of the Pines at Evercreech, I was on duty as a porter with station foreman Mark Lambert. Donald got off the engine and with Len they came over to Mark. Donald said: 'We will have to go on our own'. Len replied: 'We are over the load for this class of engine'. Then Donald looked at Mark with a twinkle in his eye and said: 'We could take one coach off if you want'. Both Mark and Len looked amazed and started to laugh. Mark said: 'It is better to have a go'. Donald replied: 'No problem and of course we will have a go'. The train left, reaching

Shepton Mallet on time, passed Masbury one minute down and arrived at Bath Green Park on time. So history was made for the Pines Express without an assisting engine. This was only for the summer services as the class 9Fs could not be used in the winter months as there was no steam heating on the engines.

Two former Somerset & Dorset railwaymen were both working at Castle Cary station; Reg Padfield had left the S&D and was now a signalman at Castle Cary while Fred Ward was a senior checker in the goods shed at the same station. One winter's morning there was snow and ice on the roads. Reg was living at Alford and travelled to work in his Austin Seven. This particular morning Reg arrived on the road bridge going over the West of England line, but going down hill he slid on some snow and ice. His car went towards a hedge; somehow it went through it and landed on four wheels without breaking any springs. Reg composed himself and drove the car through the gateway to the road and on to the station yard. Where Reg went through the hedge in the air, the field level was six feet lower than the road. Fred Ward asked Reg, who was now drinking a cup of tea after his ordeal in the signalbox, did he think he was trying to go over one of the fences on the Grand National course? Reg was not amused.

Remembering the bad weather, I recall 27th December 1962; when the snow came, it lasted until March. I walked from my home at Shepton Montague to Cole station. Arriving at Cole I went to the

Three smartly dressed railwaymen on the down platform at Evercreech New in the 1950s. Left to right, relief signalman Reg Padfield, station-master Reg Jeans and young porter Albert Attwood. (*Gerry White*)

signalbox and asked the signalman if there were any trains or light engines about. He told me that a light engine would be arriving shortly. When the engine eventually came I asked the driver could he drop me off at Evercreech Junction where I was now station foreman. On arriving at the station my main duty was to make sure the station staff were clearing the snow away on the platforms and footbridge and that the fires in the waiting rooms were kept going, and also to ensure that the water columns didn't freeze over.

I also carried out the passenger shunting duties at the station. One day, whilst detaching an engine which arrived at Evercreech off the 11.40am Bournemouth West, I had an accident. I stood up to detach the engine from the coaches and was somehow squeezed between them. My shoulders were trapped between the coach corridor and the tender. The driver of the engine was Dennis Norris, the JP from Temple-combe shed. I reported what had happened to Mr. Stowe and my doctor was called from Castle Cary. The stationmaster got me a taxi from the Junction Garage to take me home. I was off work until March. After I returned to work, Mr. Stowe had to give me a caution for not carrying out the correct rules of shunting.

The future of the Somerset & Dorset Railway was not looking that good; I saw a position going at Castle Cary at the Water Works as an engine attendant, so I applied for the post and got the job. I left the S&D in 1963, about three years before it closed; I have some very happy memories of the line and some friendships which still last to this day.

(*above*) A lovely scene and a reminder of the past at Evercreech New, as a young girl complete with pram and doll awaits the Bath train with her younger brother. Are they waiting for their dad coming off the train? They must now be in their late 40s. (*Keith Barrett collection*)

(*below*) The shadows are lengthening as 2P No.40698 hauls a train of five LMS coaches in early BR livery through Evercreech New station. (*Vic Freak collection*)

A very early photograph of Evercreech Junction station. The staff are posing for the camera, as a member of the footplate crew in the background is topping-up his thirsty engine. (*Keith Barrett collection*)

Colin Brine

On leaving school at 15 years of age in 1952, all I wanted to do was go to sea and travel the world. But in order to do this you had to be 16, so that meant finding a job for a year. My father Jim was a shunter at Evercreech Junction and he told me that there was a junior porter's job going at the Junction. After an interview with stationmaster Mr. Jack Pike the job was mine. It was a two shift system; the pay was £1.17.6d for a six-day week morning shift and £2.2.6d for the late shift. On our shift was foreman Mark Lambert, porter Bill Pippin and signal lampman Vic Freak. The Junction was well serviced for refreshments; 100yds up the road was the coach café which was an old railway coach, turned into a successful transport café by Mrs. Matthews and her daughters. Any passengers with time on their hands could be sure of a cup of tea and a snack. Alternatively just outside the gate of the up platform was the *Railway Hotel*, for some reason now called *The Natterjack Inn*. The *Railway Hotel* was run by the Jewell family. It was a favourite with many of the S&D men.

We were very proud to be one of the best kept stations, with quite a number of flower beds, for which most of the praise should go to foreman Ern Phillips or 'Green Fingers' as he was called. Junior porter's duties were varied. Firstly we saw that passengers were cared for and when trains arrived, we would unload parcels and any other goods from the guard's van. Sometimes there were goats on their way south and also calves that were wrapped in hessian with their head and legs sticking out. On the morning shift I had to go to all the oil lamps on the station, filling them up with paraffin, cleaning the globe and trimming the wick. You also had to clean the glass on the outside of all of them; there were at least 18. On the late shift they all had to be lit; this was carried out with a lighter that consisted of a brass tube filled with paraffin and a tar lashing to serve as a wick. On a wet and windy night this was quite a difficult task.

One job each morning was to take down the numbers of all wagons waiting for repairs in the sidings, and then take any mail to the two shunting yards and the North signalbox. Signalboxes were always good places to visit, nice and warm and always very clean. The brass was very shiny and gleaming, a credit to the men who worked in them. Back at the station there were always the waiting rooms to clean, platforms to sweep and any local parcels to deliver. Junior porters did this on a trade bike with a basket on the front to hold them.

A fine portrait of William Jewell who was the landlord of The Railway Hotel, Evercreech Junction from 1937 to 1961. His daughter Mary then took over as landlady for a further three years. How many pints must they have served to thirsty S&D railwaymen over the years? (*Mary Haines collection*)

It is hard to remember what went on, as it is over 50 years ago and being only 15 years old you didn't take much in. I only stayed on for 18 months; even so I recall other staff I worked with who included Joe Kemp, Ern Stockman, Arthur Badman, Bill Harris, Tony Carroll and father and son Sid and Tom Ashman. Ironically it seemed as though the world came to the Junction, servicemen returning from all parts, tourists from all over and at the beginning of term students returning to Millfield School, with some very exotic luggage labels. Thinking back I can't remember any staff travelling to work in a car; if they did there would not have been a big enough car park. However they got there, they were a good and friendly dedicated workforce. What better way to start one's working life? When I finally got my wish to go to sea, most of my journeys started and finished at Evercreech Junction.

(*left*) An unidentified 2P on the middle road at Evercreech Junction. Next to the tender is the station foreman Vic Freak. Vic was one of the most popular men on the line. (*Vic Freak collection*)

(*right*) A good customer of the *Railway Hotel* was signalman Les Williams, seen here in Evercreech Junction South signalbox. He was a real S&D star and after a few pints, he was renowned for riding his bike and singing all the way home, and now and again falling off. (*John Eaton*)

(*left*) In front of 2251 class No.2277 at Evercreech Junction are, from left to right, driver Clarence Rawles, fireman Bill Webb, and shunters Fred Hicks and Eddie Riggs. (*Ken Atkins*)

Driver Albert Good manoeuvres the wheel to top up the water for Black 5 No.44826 at Evercreech Junction. The bicycle, trolley and handcart remind us of days gone by at a country station when steam was king. *(R.K. Blencowe collection)*

Ready to leave from Evercreech Junction is 4F No.44102 with a passenger train for Bath. Looking out of the cab is Bath Green Park driver Vic Hunt. *(Keith Barrett collection)*

(*above*) In the 1930s LMS class 2P No.563 (22C Bath) waits to leave Evercreech Junction with a down passenger train. (*Keith Barrett collection*)

(*below*) Still with a low-sided tender, 4F No.44560 leaves Evercreech Junction station with a passenger train, c.1949. This engine was one of the original batch of 4Fs built for the S&D by Armstrong Whitworth of Newcastle in 1922. (*R.K. Blencowe collection*)

(*above*) An early photo at Evercreech Junction of a very clean 4-4-0 No.70 with a train for Bath. Note SDJR on the buffer beam. I wonder what type of van that is directly behind the tender? (*Richard Dagger collection*)

(*below*) On Whit Monday 18 May 1964 this excursion (1X07) left Bath at 09.35 for Bournemouth. Here we see the train leaving Evercreech Junction behind Standard class 5 No.73049 after having its assisting engine 8F No.48660 detached; this can be seen on the left on the up road. (*Alan Mitchard*)

(*above*) Driver Harry Pearce fills up with water on a Johnson class 1P No.58086 at Evercreech Junction, before working a return branch line train back to Highbridge and probably a pint of beer and a Woodbine in his local. (*Paul Strong*)

(*above*) Templecombe driver Fritz Lawrence keeps a sharp look out for the right away at Evercreech Junction whilst working north on Standard class 4 No.76056. Note this engine has a high BR 1B tender with a 4,725 gallon water capacity. (*Alan Mitchard*)

(*below*) An unidentified 2P and Battle of Britain class No.34109, *Sir Trafford-Leigh Mallory,* on the northbound Pines at Evercreech Junction in March 1951. Young porter Fred Hicks looks on as various railway personnel survey the scene. The reason for all the activity was because this was the first working of this class on the S&D. (*S.C. Townroe/R.K. Blencowe collection*)

(*above*) Malcolm Cockerell looks out from the cab of 3F No.43248 as it passes the yard at Evercreech Junction in the summer of 1956. (*Keith Barrett collection*)

(*below*) Standard class 5 No.73092 runs into Evercreech Junction with the 15.40 Bournemouth to Bristol up semi-fast. This train had priority over any other on the Dorset. (*Alan Mitchard*)

(*above*) Another photograph of the 1956 film BR Emergency Single Line Working, but quite an unusual one. The stations used were Binegar and Shepton Mallet, which were called for the film Boiland and Averton Hammer. Here we see pilotman Jim Gould on a Standard class 4 No.75071 acknowledging crossing keeper David Brooks, which we think was taken at Lamyatt Crossing. (*Norman Brooks collection*)

(*above*) Enjoying his pipe is Walter Charles Thick who was the crossing keeper here at Bruton Road and was formerly a shunter at Evercreech Junction, c.1925. (*John Thick collection*)

(*below*) A slightly misty view of class 2251 No.2218, possibly with a down branch train from Highbridge, between Lamyatt and Wyke Champflower, north of Cole. (*Paul Strong*)

(*above*) A Bath-bound stopper from Bournemouth, seen here crossing Bridge No.119, Cole Viaduct. The motive power hauling this train is class 4 No.76011. (*Paul Strong*)

(*below*) The swan song years are seen in this superb picture near Cole of a double-headed train, with pilot engine 2P No.40564 and an unidentified Standard 5 hauling an express to Bournemouth. (*Paul Strong*)

A grand view of 4F No.44248 assisting 7F No.53801 around the curves north of Cole, possibly with the down Cleethorpes-Exmouth train on 2nd July 1955, crossing bridge No.117, Wyke Lane Bridge. (*Keith Barrett collection*)

Not a thing out of place as BR Standard class 5 No.73050 enters Cole with the 9.40am Sheffield to Bournemouth West express. *(Paul Strong)*

(*above*). A very old postcard of the stationmaster and his wife outside the station house at Cole. I wonder who they are and when it was taken? (*Keith Barrett collection*)

2nd-SINGLE	SINGLE-2nd
Glastonbury & Street to	
Glastonbury & St. Cole	Glastonbury & St Cole
COLE	
(W) 2/11 Fare 2/11 (W)	
For conditions see over	or conditions see over

5237   5237

(*left*) On the footplate of BR class 4 No.75071 are driver Fred Fisher (left) and fireman Ken Stokes on a train bound for Evercreech Junction. (*Ken Stokes collection*)

(*above*) LMS class 2P No.635 speeds through Cole on a down express, c.1949. This could possibly be the Pines Express as it has carriage boards on some of its train. This site is now a housing estate. (*Keith Barrett collection*)

(*below*) Swiftly running through Cole station with a Manchester-Bournemouth express in July 1947 is LMS Stanier Black 5 No.4945. (*Keith Barrett collection*)

(*above*) An unidentified LMS 3F with a goods train between Wincanton and Cole. The footplate man George Welch smiles to the photographer as his picture is being taken. (*George Welch collection*)

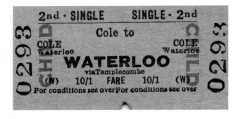

(*left*) At the controls of a GWR Pannier Tank is the late S&D footplate man Rodney Scovell. He was a renowned railway photographer and showed many slide and film shows around the country. (*Rodney Scovell collection*)

(*above*) 4F No.44558 sporting a fine plume of smoke, ambles across the Wincanton countryside with a goods train. What a splendid place to take photographs. (*Paul Strong*)

(*right*) It is high summer at Wincanton as a train from Bath to Bournemouth, headed by 2P No.40698, approaches the platform in July 1959. (*John Cornelius*)

A view taken from Wincanton footbridge looking north towards Bath. The permanent way looks in fine fettle and note the sprinkling of snow. Also the white lines on the platform have been freshly painted. Brian Taylor, the young lad on the right, is enjoying his visit to the station. His father Len took this picture and many other excellent railway photographs around Wincanton. Thank goodness he did. (*Len Taylor*)

(*right*) 3F No.43436 enters Wincanton station on 4th July 1959 with a short Highbridge to Templecombe passenger train. (*John Cornelius*)

(*below*) At the head of the train and steaming freely is Standard class 5 No.73051 with West Country No.34046, *Braunton* (now at West Somerset Railway), as they enter Wincanton station with an express on 15 April 1963. (*John Cornelius*)

(*above*) Under the bridge of the SR main line is an unidentified class Standard 4 on a down train at Templecombe Lower platform. (*Roger Holmes/Hugh Davies collection*)

(*left*) Now and again it is great to find an unusual S&D photograph and I think this one is a classic, taken at Templecombe Lower yard sidings, from Bridge 152A, of a GWR 0-6-0 Pannier Tank. The chickens belonged to the adjoining Rectory Farm on the right owned by Farmer Duck. Railway staff were known to go there and collect eggs for their breakfast. The ground was made up of ash and dust and it was an ideal place for the chickens to lay their eggs. (*Paul Strong*)

Standard class 5 No.73054 runs past Templecombe No.2 signalbox and climbs up into the Upper station ahead of the 9.30am ex-Bristol Temple Meads to Bournemouth. In the foreground is the start of the single track to Stalbridge. On the right are the tracks into Lower Yard. (*Paul Strong*)

A photograph of 2Ps Nos 40700 and 40563 standing together inside Templecombe shed. (*Wally Arnott collection*)

(*above*) The footplate crew look out from the cab of 0-6-0 Scottie goods No.2887 at Templecombe. Built at Vulcan Foundry in 1880 as No.42, the loco gave over 52 years service before she was retired. This photograph was taken on 7th June 1930 and the loco still looks in good working order. (*H.C. Casserley*)

(*below*) Activity on the track, as 2P No.40696 is off the road on the catch points at Templecombe. Some of the staff in the scene includes permanent way men Charlie Coffin, Bernard Curtis, Bill West, Bill Candy, shunter Jim Cull, stationmaster Bill Newman and station inspector Alan Rice. (*Ian Matthews collection*)

(*above*) Formerly S&DJR No.72, 3F No.43216 is seen in 1962 waiting for the signals outside Templecombe station. Looking towards the photographer are fireman Cliff Day (left) and driver George Eason. (*Keith Barrett collection*)

(*below*) A group photo in front of No. 41283 at Templecombe shed in 1957, left to right, steamraiser Walt Webb, fitter's mate Bert Rolls, coalman Ern Cawley, fitter Ken Arnott and labourer Vic Lephard. (*Keith Barrett collection*)

(*above*) With the light shining through on a lovely day at Templecombe station, W.H. Smith's kiosk manager Charlie Gosling poses for the camera, c.1950s. (*Keith Barrett collection*)

(*left*) Staff enjoying a game of cards outside Templecombe signalbox in the 1920s. Second and third from the left are, Billy Bow and Fred Hatchley. (*Keith Barrett collection*)

(*right*) Steamraiser Walt Webb in the stores at Templecombe shed in 1962. He is holding a bundle of white cloths which were issued every two days to drivers and firemen before leaving the shed. Former S&D fireman Keith Barrett recalls his mother was always happy to have these, as they made wonderful floor cloths. (*Gordon Webb collection*)

(*below*) Dolly Sanger smiles across the counter at Templecombe station buffet. Fresh flowers adorn the counter and everything looks sparkling. (*Ian Matthews collection*)

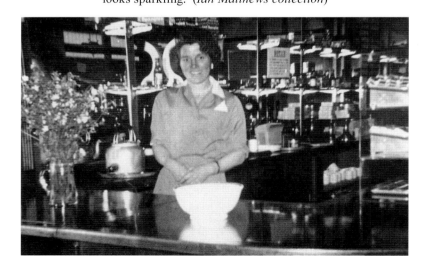

(*above*) Driver Ron Luckins and Joe Paddick of Salisbury depot wait at Templecombe shed with No.35028 *Clan Line* to work the last special off the S&D back to Waterloo on 6th March 1966. (*John Cornelius*)

(*above*) Fitter's mate Frank Ray on Templecombe shed filling the lubricator on a Standard class 4 before the loco was hauled to Ringwood for scrapping on 6th March 1966. (*Keith Barrett collection*)

(*below*) In front of a class 4 No.75072 at Templecombe is driver Johnny Walker (left) and fireman Tony White who are in between turns, before returning to Bournemouth. (*John Cornelius*)

(*below*) With the coal crane out of action, labourer Vic Lephard coals Ivatt Tank No.41283 by hand on Templecombe shed. Looking on and ready to help out is driver Ray Stokes. (*Ian Matthews collection*)

(*right*) Two signal and telegraph railwaymen from Exeter who are carrying their overcoats, are in conversation with Templecombe men, inspector Bert Dray (second on the left) and Fred Sanger. (*Keith Barrett collection*)

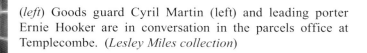

(*left*) Goods guard Cyril Martin (left) and leading porter Ernie Hooker are in conversation in the parcels office at Templecombe. (*Lesley Miles collection*)

(*right*) Taken in the Royal Hotel, Templecombe. From left to right, Brian Tanner, driver Art Hatcher, Ray Darke and fireman Gordon Hatcher. Note they were all smokers; Art always smoked Craven A. (*Keith Barrett collection*)

(*left*) Seen at Templecombe Lower yard in the 1960s are fireman Cliff Day (left) and driver Art Hatcher. (*Gerald Box*)

(*above*) Guard Albert (Dickie) Bird always gets a mention in my books. What a lovely surprise when his daughter from Canada sent me this excellent photograph of him, with his good friend, driver Albert Good on the right, c.1940s. Dickie was a keen rose grower and when the train stopped at stations like Shillingstone he would pop out of his guard's van with his secateurs and give the station roses a good prune. (*Maureen Carroll collection*)

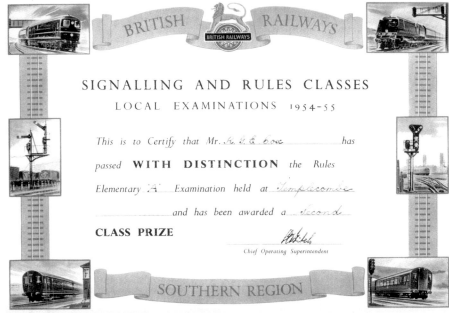

BRITISH RAILWAYS

BRITISH RAILWAYS

SIGNALLING AND RULES CLASSES

LOCAL EXAMINATIONS 1954-55

This is to Certify that Mr. *R. G. E. Cox* has

passed **WITH DISTINCTION** the Rules

Elementary 'A' Examination held at *Templecombe*

and has been awarded a *second*

CLASS PRIZE

Chief Operating Superintendent

SOUTHERN REGION

(*left*) What a splendid certificate issued by British Railways to Ron Cox at Templecombe over half a century ago. (*Maureen Carroll collection*)

85

Not strictly S&D, but an early 1900s view of Templecombe (LSWR) looking towards Gillingham. The gentleman on the left is Ern Garrett. The tools he is carrying suggest he could have been a lengthman or even a wheeltapper. (*Author's collection*)

(*above*) Permanent way man Archie Sutton looks a lonely figure as he walks on the track at Common Lane Crossing in the 1950s. (*Keith Barrett collection*)

(*right*) Guard Hugh Berryman holding the family's pet cat on the track at Park Lane Crossing where he lived with his wife Mabel who was the crossing keeper here. (*Joan Fisher collection*)

8F No.48660 moves freight from Bath Green Park through Templecombe station to the goods yard. (*Paul Strong*)

Family photographs taken at Henstridge station in August 1940.

(*above*) Husband and wife team of stationmaster Jack and Edna Dulborough. They lived in the station house which is still there today. (*Jack Dulborough collection*)

(*right*) In this photo Jack Dulborough is playing with the family's pet dog Tim. The wooden building behind had a coal-fired boiler and was used for baths. (*Edna Dulborough*)

(*below*) In August 1940, Jack Dulborough, holding a shunting pole, enjoys having his photo taken on the platform. Note the hand crane in the background. (*Edna Dulborough*)

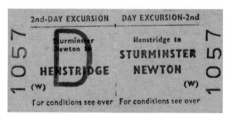

(*below*) Driver John Dray reversing a class 2P 4-4-0. He enjoyed a pint or two with his work mates and was a stalwart of Templecombe shed. His father Bert was an inspector on the S&D. (*John Dray collection*)

London Midland and Scottish Railway Company.—TELEGRAM.

Ballast tomorrow 5 30 am Ibombe to Barly Gate working between No 2 and Henstridge on the forward journey

(*above*) Standard 4 No.76027 with a Yeovil Junction to Poole freight on the border of Somerset and Dorset. In the background is Landshire Lane Bridge No.161, which is situated between Henstridge and Stalbridge. (*Paul Strong*)

(*below*) Standard class 4 No.76025 engulfed in smoke and steam leaves Henstridge with a passenger train in January 1965. Look at the scrap vehicles on the right. How much would they be worth today in good working order? (*Paul Strong*)

BR Standard 4MT No.75072 trundles gently through Henstridge with the 11.40 Bournemouth West train to Bath Green Park in March 1965. (*Paul Strong*)

Between Stalbridge and Henstridge is Standard class 4 No.76015 with a three-coach up local near Landshire Lane Bridge No.161. When I received this photograph I was unsure of where it was. So Keith Barrett and Paul Guppy who live nearby went on a recce and tracked the exact position of the train. They found the withy trees in the background and also the round bush above coach two, which was right next to Stalbridge yard. (*Paul Strong*)

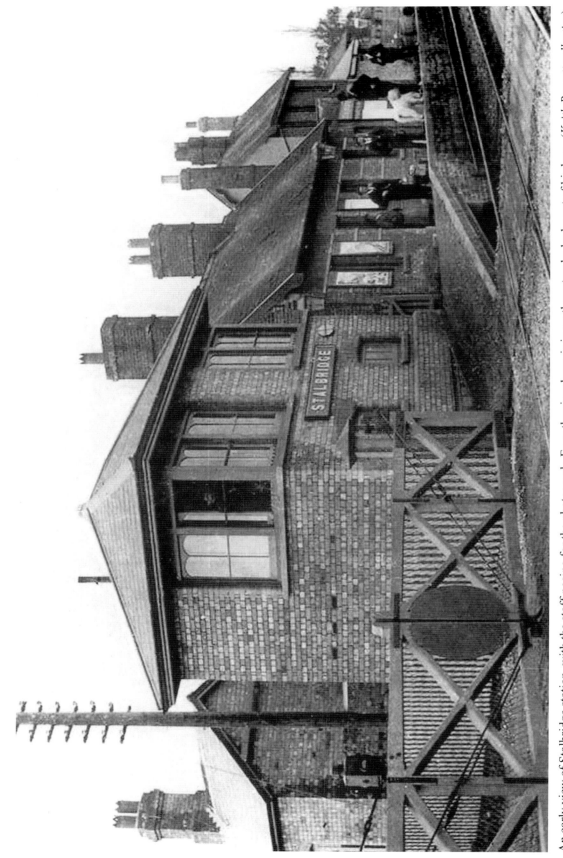

An early view of Stalbridge station, with the staff posing for the photograph. Even the signalman is in on the act as he looks out of his box. (*Keith Barrett collection*)

(*above*) Branksome driver Donald Beale, who spent 47 years on the S&D, looks out from the cab of Standard 4 No.75073 at Stalbridge in the 1960s. (*Paul Strong*)

(*above*) Donald's mate for the trip on 75073 is Bournemouth Central fireman Ron Whittaker who is pictured here. (*Paul Strong*)

(*right*) A rare photograph of staff at Stalbridge, c.1960. From left to right, unknown, signalman Robert (Jock) Mckennie, stationmaster Sydney Cox, booking clerk Roy Scammell and porter Chris Mitchell. Sydney Cox started on the railway in March 1914 and retired in September 1964. He was also the stationmaster at other stations on the S&D and came to Stalbridge in 1947. His son Alan continued the family name on this railway as a signalman. (*Alan Cox collection*)

(*above*) On a bright spring day in April 1965 a class 2 No.41243 leaves Stalbridge with the 17.30 Bournemouth West to Templecombe train. (*Paul Strong*)

(*below*) I hope the fireman on BR class 4 No.80059 can catch, as Stalbridge signalman Alan Cox throws him the tablet. Well done to Paul Strong for taking this marvellous photograph in 1965. (*Paul Strong*)

(*above*) 4F No.44560 has a clear road through Stalbridge with the 15.03 freight from Poole to Yeovil Junction. Note the brakevan at the front and rear of the train, necessitated by the reversal at Templecombe. (*Paul Strong*)

(*below*) A great close up shot of Standard 4 No.75073, on a down freight at Stalbridge in 1965. The Templecombe driver in the cab is Walt Jeans, one of the top link drivers for many years on the S&D. He was a lovely fellow whom I had the pleasure to meet on several occasions.

Pat Holmes

In 1959 I started on the S&D at Blandford Forum as a junior porter, working with Walt Warren. I had to work different shifts, so there was many a time I had to ride the 10 miles home to Sturminster on my bicycle in the dark. I only stayed at Blandford for a short while before being transferred to Sturminster Newton.

During my spell at Sturminster there was a tablet failure and the stationmaster Wally Gilbert was required to act as a pilot. I was told he had gone to the bank and to find him immediately. With the two trains waiting in Sturminster Newton station it was a matter of urgency that I found him. After running up and down the High Street I found him in the British Legion. He told me not to say anything to anybody, which I never did.

Templecombe driver Fritz Lawrence looks out of the cab of class 5 No.73054. Fritz was a bookmaker and was always keen to give you tips on horse racing and was also ready to collect bets off many railwaymen. (*Alan Mitchard*)

I then moved on to Templecombe Motive Power depot as a cleaner and assisted Norman Penhaligon, the boilersmith. Within a short time I was soon learning how to fire an engine. My first firing turn was with Ben Dyer, a real comedian and a joy to work with. We only had to get a couple of engines ready as our train to Bailey Gate had been cancelled. Another driver I worked with for many months was Bert Jones who taught me the art of firing. We became good mates and had some eventful journeys. We took 9F No.92220 *Evening Star* on her first journey on the S&D on the early mail to Hamworthy, working back the 10.05 Bournemouth West to Bradford.

When we were under the control of the Western Region, Art Hatcher and I had to go to Plymouth for a medical. I got the blame for Art failing his medical due to high blood pressure; drinking all the way on the train did not help. Art was put on shunting duties until his blood pressure was reduced. For a time I worked with Pat Evans who knew the rule book backwards. One day we were shunting at Templecombe Lower yard moving loaded coal wagons, when the rails spread and about 10 wagons were running on the sleepers. Pat just said: 'Not our fault'.

On another occasion, after changing with a Bath crew, we were returning from Shepton Mallet with a goods train to Evercreech. Upon reaching Evercreech, the guard, Brian (Kipper) Padfield, came storming down to the engine shouting to Pat: 'Don't you know the rules. I've been putting my brake on and off to attract your attention because I left my guard's bag at Shepton'.

I recall the bad winter of 1962/3. It was the time when everything was snowed up. On the Saturday night there was a blizzard; by Sunday morning at day-break we had four feet of snow. I was booked as a fireman to work the Bailey Gate milk from Templecombe. I walked the 10 miles to Templecombe from my home at Sturminster, arriving at 13.50, well in time to book on at 14.10. I remember the time because Harry Jeans the shedmaster told me the time as I arrived. My driver was Trevor Nettley and we had an Ivatt class 2 Tank engine No.41241. We set off with about four empty milk tanks and a guard's van. Snow drifts were deeper than the height of the engine in places, but the snow being still powdery allowed us to push through. On arriving at Stalbridge we picked up the Shillingstone signalman Alan Cox whose father Sydney was the stationmaster at Stalbridge. Against all regulations, off we went through the deep snow. I had to hold on to Alan to stop him jumping off the footplate; he said he could not see the rails, nor could we. About a mile before Sturminster Newton there was a cutting about 10 feet deep and full to the top with snow. My father was watching us go through the cutting and out of sight until we reappeared through 20-foot-deep drifts. We dropped Alan off at Shillingstone and we carried on to Bailey Gate into chaos; all the roads were blocked and no staff were at the milk factory. There was a shortage of milk as it was all frozen. We returned later that day to Templecombe, picking up Alan Cox from Shillingstone and returning him to Stalbridge station. When we stopped at Sturminster Newton station my dad was there with hot steaming cups of tea for us. We arrived back at 22.00 just in time for a couple of pints. I stayed the night in the messroom at Templecombe. It was unbelievable on the way back, to see the depth of snow we had to cut through without a snow plough.

On the Monday we were on a Tank engine with a snow plough with two tender engines trying to keep the line open. We drew lots to see who worked on the warmest engine, which was our Tankie. I got home on Wednesday, as Harry Jeans gave me the day off. I was back on the plough for the rest of the week.

On the Saturday I booked on at 16.00 with George Welch, with a passenger train to Evercreech Junction to relieve the day gang along with Pat Evans, Dave Walters, Dick Howcutt and another fireman who I think was Bill Silk. We arrived at Evercreech to find the plough engine was damaged and would have to return to Templecombe. I put the engine away and asked where George was and was told he had gone. So I caught the next train back to Sturminster Newton and was home by 20.00. After a wash and change I went into the *Rivers Arms* until closing time. Sunday dinnertime I was back in the pub when Dave Walters came in; he also lived in Sturminster. He informed me that I was booked off at 05.00 that morning. George had gone back to Evercreech and not home as I had thought. Nothing was ever said to me officially.

Over the years working on the Somerset & Dorset Railway I worked and met many men like Ron Spiller, Brendan Scott, Jack Bell, Peter Pike, John Wood, Gordon Hatcher, Alf and Mick Elliott, Maurice Stacey, George Merchant, Frank and Reg Staddon, Tosh Hardy and many more. I was sorry when the S&D closed, but memories of those great times, working with great mates, will always be with me.

This is one of those S&D staff photographs where you wish you knew who they were, what station they are from, and when it was taken. Has anybody got any ideas? (*Keith Barrett collection*)

(*above*) The signalman has already put the tablet in its catcher, as 8F No.48706 roars through Sturminster Newton with the up Great Western Society Rail Tour special on 5 March 1966. (*John Pearce collection*)

(*left*) Motor Trolley No.59 and driver crossing the River Stour on what could be Bridge No.175, Fiddleford Mill, situated between Sturminster Newton and Shillingstone. (*S.C. Townroe/R.K. Blencowe collection*)

(*above*) On parade in a very early photograph, are the stationmaster and eight members of the Shillingstone station team. Note the two ladies in period dress on the left. Stationmasters who worked here include Mr. Courage 1876-1914, George Coles 1923-1933, Ken Davey 1965 and Ken Forrester 1965-1966. (*Keith Barrett collection*)

(*right*) Photographs like this remind us that the S&D was built on the staff who helped make this such a close-knit family railway, no more so than at Shillingstone station where this was taken in 1963. The smartly dressed railwaymen are, in the back row from left to right, goods porter Harry Guy; my very good friend, porter Bob Downes; and relief porter Ron Jackson. In the front row are signalman George Ainsworth; stationmaster Sydney Cox; and booking clerk Donald Ridout. (*Bob Downes collection*)

(*above*) Who are the lovely ladies waiting for a train at Shillingstone in 1965? They must now be in their fifties. (*C.L. Caddy*)

(*below*) Two members of the same type, WC No.34006 *Bude* and BB No.34057 *Biggin Hill*, with an LCGB Somerset & Dorset Rail Tour going over the River Stour, Blandford on 5th March 1966. The reflection on the water is stunning, and it is one of those photographs which makes you wish you were there. (*Keith Barrett collection*)

(*above*) Ivatt 2-6-2T No.41243 stops for water at Blandford with the 12.23pm Templecombe to Bournemouth down local. (*Keith Barrett collection*)

(*below*) After 41 years of loyal service to the Somerset & Dorset Railway, Blandford Forum porter Walter Warren retired in October 1961. At his retirement presentation are his workmates, from left to right, porter Roy Yates, signalman Arthur Bowen, booking clerk Len Farley, shunter Ivor (Ginger) Ridout, booking clerk Derek Edge with Walter Warren receiving his barometer from stationmaster Arthur Powis. S&D photographs like this remind us that people retired gracefully in those days; unfortunately this doesn't always happen in today's world. (*Graham O'Donnell collection*)

A fine view of Blandford Forum station. The whole station looks immaculate with the 27-lever signalbox on the left-hand side. It was a busy station with a lot of traffic coming from the nearby Army Camp; Hall and Woodhouse; Flight Refuelling; and Hanford, Croft House, Bryanston and Clayesmore schools. It was a station full of S&D characters like Joe Penny, Ivor Ridout, Roy White, father and son Charlie and Harold (Nobby) Whiting, Les Barlick, Vic Beale, Eddie Caines, Jeff Seaman, Don Newman, Pat Holmes and many more. (*R.K. Blencowe collection*)

(*inset*) An S&D postcard depicting Blandford Market Place (*Author's collection*)

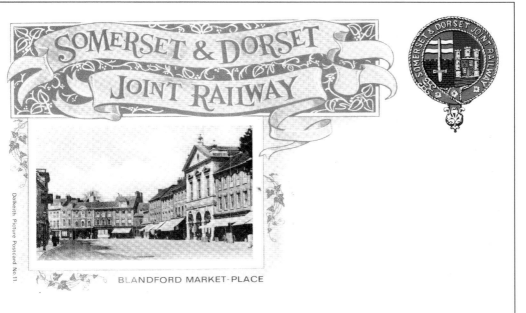

SOMERSET & DORSET JOINT RAILWAY

Dalkeith Picture Postcard No 11

BLANDFORD MARKET-PLACE

(*left*) A wonderfully atmospheric photograph, but a sad occasion – the last down train at Blandford Forum with BR 2-6-4MT No.80138 on 5th March 1966. On the right, shunter Ivor (Ginger) Ridout views the scene with a sad heart, after giving over 20 years' service to the line. Note the wreath on the smokebox and the Waterloo sign. (*Joe Robbins*)

(*right*) It looks like a staged scene for the photographer, as BR class 4 No.80019 stands in Blandford Forum station. The Bournemouth Central driver looks out of the cab with shunter Ivor (Ginger) Ridout also in attendance. This photo was taken on 14th September 1966, six months after closure of the line to passenger traffic. Note the discs on the front; these were used in place of headlamps on the Southern Region. (*Paul Strong*)

(*left*) Caught hard at work is class 5 No.73068 as it makes its way through Charlton Marshall halt in 1965. (*J.W.T. House/ C.L. Caddy collection*)

(*above*) Is it an S&D station garden or is he in his own home? This lovely photograph of a guard looking extremely smart in full regalia, also begs a couple of questions: when was this taken and more importantly who is this gentleman? (*SDRT collection*)

(*above*) A team photo at Bailey Gate. On the West Country is driver Bert Freakley and fireman Bert Short; on the platform, from left to right, signalman Walt Hart, inspector Jack Hookey, stationmaster Mr. M.L. Jones and guard Albert (Dickie) Bird. (*Bert Short collection*)

(*right*) On the platform at Bailey Gate are boxes of watercress waiting to be loaded, while on the footplate of West Country No.34037 *Clovelly*, are Bert Freakley and Bert Short. (*Bert Short collection*)

(*right*) Driver Bert Jones is ready to head north with 7F No.53804. Note the catcher on the tender and the young lad looking over the fence next to the bridge. (*Keith Barrett collection*)

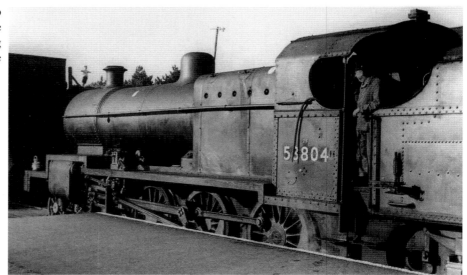

(*left*) Standard class 4 No.76026 (Blandford end, with class 3 No.77014 out of view Bournemouth end) climbs towards Corfe Mullen with the up LCGB Dorset and Hants Rail Tour on Sunday 16th October 1966. (*Keith Barrett collection*)

(*right*) On the outskirts of Broadstone in 1950, is 7F No.53803 hauling a Bath passenger train. The footplateman George Welch leans out of the cab to make sure he is in the picture. (*H.F. Wheeller/R.S. Carpenter collection*)

(*right*) A steamy affair with 9F No.92233. In front of the 2-10-0 are, from left to right, guard Stan Cherret?, driver Donald Beale, fireman Ron Hyde and driver Jim Tranter. (*John Eaton*)

(*below*) An unidentified S&DJR class 1P 0-4-4T arrives at Bournemouth West with a down train in 1928. (*Keith Barrett collection*)

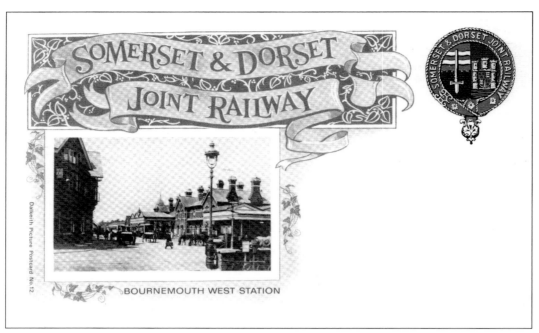

(*left*) An S&D post-card depicting Bourne-mouth West station. (*Author's collection*)

(*above right*) An im-maculate looking M7 No.30107 gets ready to leave Bournemouth West station in 1952 with a passenger train to Brockenhurst via Wimborne. (*R.K. Blencowe collection*)

(*below right*) 9F No. 92001 stands ready to move from Bourne-mouth West with a passenger train. On the left a young trainspotter gazes at the vast engine. I wonder if he cabbed the loco? (*Keith Barrett collection*)

(*below*) A very old photograph of Bournemouth West station, c.1900s. Note the period dress and no cars on view. (*Richard Dagger collection*)

Keith Barrett

In the 1950s I was working as a cleaner doing shift work at Templecombe shed. After only a short period of time I went on to the footplate. This was due to a shortage of staff being off sick, summer holidays, Territorial Army training and the increase in trains to cover the summer service. Also there were men being transferred to other depots to get their grades as firemen. At one time the shed lost Wilfred Jeans, Bob Jeans, Den Matthews and Ken Doggerell, who all transferred to Salisbury shed, still within the Southern Region, to be upgraded. So as time passed by, it became more likely that I would soon be passed out as a cleaner, which enabled me to be called upon when required. Once I was passed out by the shedmaster Vic Vosper, it was up to me to keep an eye out for the roster chart each day. This was posted at 11.00am and put in a glass case in the signing-on lobby by the clerk, Jim Fry. It showed what changes were being made to the staff to cover the next day's workings. If your name appeared on the chart, it would tell you what train you were to cover. There was also a call-boy who would come knocking on your door to give you a calling out ticket.

You had to work all shifts throughout the day and night and at short notice. I recall travelling spare to Bath, then working a Saturday express with Bath driver Dick Evry to Gloucester and back. We had a 2-6-0 (nicknamed Crab) on the outward journey and a Standard class 5 for the return journey. On this trip we stopped at Bath Junction for me to carry out rule 55 owing to the station being blocked with an up Bournemouth express. Once the road was cleared we ran on into Bath station. It was there that we were both relieved and I returned home to Templecombe as a passenger, tired out. This was an enjoyable trip as Dick Evry was such a likeable character and it is a journey that I will always remember.

On another occasion with driver Reg Burt we had to go spare to Branksome shed and take a light engine, which was a 4F No.44560 to Bournemouth West station. After coupling up to the stock of 10 coaches we worked a special to Highbridge and returned light engine, arriving back at Templecombe around midnight. What a long day that was.

I do remember once having a joke played on me; I had been out late to a dance and I was on duty at 3.20am with driver Ben Dyer to work the 4.20am

freight to Evercreech Junction. On arrival in the down sidings he told me to go and get my head down in the messroom, as I was not feeling very well, whilst he carried on the shunting in the yard. Unbeknown to me he had tied my boot laces to the locker doors. When I woke up I went to get up and fell over and hit my head on the table. They had to give me First Aid which resulted in me having a large bandage around my head for the rest of the day.

We had turns which we covered over the branch to Highbridge and the Wharf. One of the turns was to work the 6.05am from Evercreech Junction up sidings to Highbridge; I did this on numerous occasions. You had to get up very early to sign on at 3.50am, then off to Templecombe Upper yard, making sure you had your lunch bag, tea can and hand brush. Then it was a ride in the rear brakevan of the 4.20am freight to Evercreech Junction. On arrival you then had to walk in the dark to the up sidings and relieve the fireman, Derek (Tanker) Jones or Bill Webb, on the yard shunter at 5.15am. This would be a MR class 3F 0-6-0 known as a Bulldog and was very often No.43216 or No.43427. Already on the engine would be the night shift driver Cecil Cooper. He was to be relieved at 6.00am by driver Donald Webb who would be my mate for the day. In the yard marshalling our train was the head shunter George Green; other shunters there included Malcolm Hatherell and Fred Hicks. When the train had been completed our guard Frank Packer walked along and inspected and recorded all of the wagons to make sure they were fit to run. Also he made sure that all of the hand brakes were in the off position. He would then tell the driver the load of the train before returning to the rear brakevan. Looking for the ground signal (dummy) in the off position, the guard would then signal to the crew a green light for the right away. So off you would go along the curve of the neck which ran behind Evercreech Junction North signalbox, collecting the tablet from the signalman Bill Harris along the way (these tablets were made of alloy and if you didn't catch yours correctly and it hit your knuckles then, my God, did it hurt for a few days afterwards). At the end of the neck another dummy will be in the off position and allow the driver out to join up with the branch main line to Highbridge. Whilst moving forward and now picking up speed, the fireman would be looking back to the brakevan to see the guard waving a white light or his arm (in daylight) to indicate that the train was complete. The fireman would give the same signal back to the guard and the driver would give a short sharp whistle from the engine to signal the go ahead.

Now it is all eyes forward as the train goes past the advance starting signal and the down sidings where the head shunter Charlie Vaughan is busy marshalling the 6.35am freight to Poole, which will be hauled by a 7F 2-8-0. Going under Park Bridge (No.242) which carries the road to Allen's Farm and a public footpath, on the right you can see the church tower at Evercreech New and the Mendip Hills. Ahead just on a left-hand bend is Elbow Corner Crossing which has a semaphore stop signal on each side operated by Mrs. Toose the crossing keeper. Now running at the maximum speed of 40mph, it is time to ease off gently, ready for the descent down Pylle Bank. On shutting the damper to allow the fire to die down and the injector on to maintain a full boiler of water, the driver closes the regulator and drops the reversing lever into full forward gear. This lets the weight of the train push the engine forward as the driver applies the vacuum brake to stop the train from running away. At the rear the guard will also be applying his brake to control the rear half of the train.

Running under Pylle Station Bridge (No.243) (which carried the road to Shepton Mallet and was demolished in 1970 by Somerset County Council) we then pass Cockmill Crossing, home of Mrs. Higgins the crossing keeper. Here Donald admires the fields and says what a lovely lot of corn there is growing alongside the railway fence, only to hear later what happened that day. Still running down the gradient the driver now observes the 15mph speed restriction. This restriction appears to have been there for years, so one can only think that

Steanbow Crossing keeper Gertrude Annie Dunkerton was in charge here for over 25 years. They were the unsung heroes of the branch, working long shifts in all weathers. (*Ray Dunkerton collection*)

the ground was very soft and unable to be maintained to the correct level. Half a mile east of West Pennard is Steanbow Crossing with Gertrude Dunkerton as the crossing keeper; the signals are pulled off. Running through West Pennard station at 6.23am, the damper is opened slightly to keep the steam and water up whilst the driver pulls the reversing lever up the rack nearly into mid-gear, and opens the regulator enough to take the strain of the couplings, to avoid a snatch. Having given up the tablet and collected a new one from the signalman Ray Gilham for the section to Glastonbury, which is collected by hand, all is in order for the driver to set the controls as required and begin to view the countryside just as daylight is breaking. Cruising over Pennard Lane Crossing and running almost in a straight line to Glastonbury, the Tor can be seen across to the left. Going under Wells Road Bridge (No.264), commonly known as Tin Bridge, we sweep around the left-hand curve soon to run alongside the adjoining trackbed to Wells, which closed on 29th October 1951. Again, the driver shuts off the steam supply and puts the reversing lever forward ready for our first stop at Glastonbury station. As the train free-wheels on we pass over Cemetery Lane Crossing, operated by Joyce Miles. Next we run under Northload Road Bridge (No.265), which carries the road to Glastonbury. With the distant signal on caution, the driver gives a long blast on the engine whistle to indicate to the signalman that he wants the road into the station. A signal check and the road is soon cleared and we are passing over Dye House Crossing, where station foreman Hughie Durston raises his arm with a wave as we stop at Glastonbury station at 6.35am. The signalman, Roy Davies, comes over to collect the tablet and returns to his box to set the road up to detach any freight wagons due for Glastonbury. With the instructions from the shunter Ken Atkins and the guard, the driver moves forward to clear the yard points. Reversing into the yard he shunts them into place at Ken's request who then unhooks the wagons, and the engine goes back to its train. The guard returns to his brakevan and the signalman hands the crew the next tablet for the section from Glastonbury to Shapwick. (I wonder what this station would have been like had it been still open during the Glastonbury Pop Festival? What a busy time that would have been.)

At 7.05am the guard gives the right away and the driver checks the signal is off as he slowly departs with his train. Turning a left-hand bend you can see the River Brue Aqueduct Bridge (No.268), then, close by, Aqueduct Crossing where Mrs. Jones is the crossing keeper. Then a little further on we pass over Sharpham Crossing with Mrs. Baker in charge. We follow the River Brue (Main Drain) alongside the track, where occasionally you will spot a heron. Across the fields the workmen are digging the peat, with rows and rows built up to dry. With the train now rolling along nicely, we pass around the curves and ahead the Ashcott distant signal is in the off position. Through Ashcott station, home to Rose and Guy Parsons – what a character he was. Another porter who worked there was Johnny Thorn. The line is now straight and in the distance you can see Alexander's Siding; this was a private siding for the Eclipse Peat Company.

It was here, on 19th August 1949, that the 8.00am mixed train from Glastonbury to Bridgwater collided with the Eclipse Peat Company's narrow-gauge petrol engine which had stalled on the crossing. The train was being hauled by 0-6-0 No.3260 (ex-SDJR No.76) and driven by Ray Stokes and fired by Sid Boussey, both from Templecombe shed. The accident happened in thick fog; luckily the crew managed to jump off before the engine derailed and berthed itself into the rhine. Having worked with Ray for a number of years there was never any mention of this accident by him.

On approaching Shapwick the driver gets his train under control in readiness to stop in the loop at 7.16am to cross the down 7.00am passenger from Highbridge. Handing the tablet to the signalman Bill Vowles we come to a stop clear of East End Crossing. The down local arrives on time with Highbridge crew, driver Bill May and fireman Tony Rossiter, at 7.18am and departs at 7.19am behind another 3F, No.43194. With the road set and the starting signal off the signalman gives the crew the tablet for the all

clear to Highbridge. Looking back the guard gives the right away and the driver moves forward on the last part of this journey. Running on at a nice steady pace we pass Catcott Crossing operated by Mrs. Seery, then pass Edington Burtle station with the Bridgwater branch swinging off to the left. Firemen Gordon Hatcher, Percy Hobbs, John Dray, Alwyn Hannam and many others used to work a lodging turn to Bridgwater, before it closed.

Now having to run the fire down, it is time to look across the Somerset levels and enjoy the beautiful views. Then over Huntspill Crossing run by Mrs. Irene Hyman, and soon over Crips Corner Bridge (No.276). The track now swings slightly to the left and the signals ahead are in the off position. We run past the Wilts United Dairies Milk Factory and through Bason Bridge station. It is now just over a mile to go before we reach Highbridge, so the damper is finally shut down with the fire doors opened and the injector kept still on, to fill up the boiler ready for arrival. The driver keeps a close watch out ready to shut off the steam supply and put the reversing lever into full forward gear. The Highbridge distant signal is on so the driver slowly brakes to slow the train down. As the home signal is off he eases the braking to coast along and slowly bring the train to a halt at 7.40am alongside the Highbridge East 'C' signalbox. Here I hand the tablet to the signalman Jock Kirkbright and prepare to change over with the incoming freight from Highbridge Wharf at 7.41am. This would then mean a change over of crews, with driver Maurice Cook and fireman John Rice taking charge of our incoming up freight and Donald and I on the footplate of the down freight with 3F No.43436. Before departing at 7.50am I go into the signalbox with my tea can and make a brew of tea to be enjoyed on the return journey. With our guard Frank Packer now in the rear brakevan of our train and all signals clear it is time for the driver to check the tablet and move off. Again, acknowledging the guard's signal the driver gradually picks up speed before slowing down for the booked stop at Bason Bridge from 7.55am until 8.05am, to pick-up two full water cans to be dropped off at Huntspill Crossing. The porter Frank Jones places the two cans on the running plate of the loco ready to be dropped off when required. Moving off again, the next stop will be at Huntspill Crossing. Whilst here, the two full cans are taken off by the crew, as this house never had any running water like many others on the line.

Another two empty cans are loaded and delivered to Edington Burtle at 8.15am. The empties are taken off by porter Tom Mogg and another two full cans loaded on. We move off at 8.17am to the next stop at Catcott Crossing. Here you only have to drop off the two full cans, and then move swiftly on, arriving at Shapwick at 8.28am. We stop in the down loop and hand the tablet to the signalman Bill Vowles. Here we wait to cross the 8.15am local from Evercreech Junction due in at 8.49am until 8.50am.

Now the road has been re-set and with another tablet from Shapwick to Glastonbury it's time to restart the train at 9.05am. Just a little further along the line and the next stop is at Alexander's Siding for the Eclipse Peat Company at 9.09am. The driver stops the train on the main line clear of the siding points. At this moment the guard walks up to the front of the train and unhooks behind any box vans that are due to be shunted off. The guard then takes the tablet from the crew and places it in the ground frame to operate the points which the driver has now cleared. Then waved back by the guard, we reverse into the siding to collect the outgoing loaded vans, hauling them forward. Then, reversing back on to its train, the guard hooks up the vans at the rear end and unhooks again to take the empty vans back into the siding for berthing, the engine being then unhooked and moved out and backed on to its train ready for the departure. The guard returns the tablet to the crew and walks back to his brakevan and gives the right away at 9.25am. The driver now continues his short run to Ashcott, again stopping at the home signal. Now with the assistance of porter Guy Parsons the guard again carries out the same procedure as at Alexander Sidings. After completion, with the tablet in the safe hands of the crew, it's time at 9.45am for the driver to head for

Driver Ronald Andrews waits on the footplate with a can of water, while his fireman, George Stent fills the crossing keeper's churn at Elbow Corner Crossing.
(Barry Andrews collection)

Glastonbury. On approaching Glastonbury the train is checked before heading into the station, giving up the tablet to the signalman Roy Davies on its route and arriving at 9.53am. When the road is set the guard waves you backwards into the down siding for berthing. He then unhooks behind any wagons that have to be dispatched into the up sidings at Glastonbury. You now make a number of shunting movements in the yard under shunter Ken Atkins' instructions. During this stopover it is time for me to be relieved by another fireman from Templecombe shed, sometimes Dave (Zippo) Young or Bill Trigg. At 10.15am you then walk across to the down platform to catch the 10.19am (9.45am ex Highbridge) back to Templecombe, arriving at 11.10am. On arrival back to the engine shed, you put your kit away into your locker and sign-off.

I found out later that on the return journey at Evercreech Junction, the yard shunter Malcolm Hatherell called out to my driver Donald Webb that he was wanted by Bath Control on the telephone. Off he goes to the shunter's cabin to hear from control that a farmer at Pylle had reported his field of corn was well ablaze and blamed Donald for working the train too heavy handed. I guess this must have been another insurance claim.

Other duties which we covered over the branch were the 'Highbridge Milky' with drivers and firemen Harry Pearce, Ronald (Chummy) Andrews, Bill May, Charlie King, Bill Parsons, Joe Prentice, Stan Bedford, George Brooks, John Baker, Terry Fry and guards Cecil Cox, Johnny Beck, Arthur Blackborrow, Jimmy Yelling, George Baker and Walter Binding. The trains on this trip were also worked by the class 3Fs Nos.43218 or 43248.

I do remember a few things we used to get up to with the permanent way men. When working a train and you spotted them ahead, the injector was put on and when you were nearly up to the men the slacken-pipe was turned on and water sprayed across the back plate and over the coal into the tender. This would send all the coal dust and black splashes over the men as you ran by. Also on the 3.05pm freight from Poole to Templecombe we would stop in a cutting near Cliff Bridge, between Stourpaine and Shillingstone. Laid out up the bank would be bundles of pea and bean sticks which the permanent way gang had made. So several bundles were put up into the tender and taken to the shed ready to be carried home.

Another time we were drinking in *The Half Moon* at Horsington until 1.00am with my brother-in-law Den Morgan and his mates. One of them was Gordon Fudge who was drunk and singing away, 'Rabbits in the pea patch'. He had to be at work at 3.45am to work on an engineer's train and was being picked up at Cheriton Crossing. We stopped the train and he gingerly got into the front brakevan and away we headed to Midsomer Norton. When it was time for the permanent way gang to start work, Gordon got up into a wagon of Meldon dust with his shovel and worked away all day, none the worse for wear. What a constitution he had.

Once I was made up to a fireman, my wages went up to £2.2.6d per week and I was then allowed to work in Nos.1 and 2 links from Templecombe shed, working the 8.20am local to Highbridge and returning with the 2.20pm local to Templecombe, worked by a Johnson Tank class 1P, Nos.58047, 58072 or 58086. The 4.05pm local to Highbridge normally had an Ivatt Tank class 2P, either No.41248 or 41249; we would then return with the 6.15pm 'Highbridge Market'.

From then on I worked as a full time fireman with driver Ray Stokes.

This turned out to be a happy time and a wonderful experience for me. I recall working with Ray one Christmas. We worked back on the 10.18am from Hamworthy to Broadstone with a class 7F and brakevan. We would have the right away and go like hell to gain a few minutes before stopping in section. We would get off the engine with the coal-pick and firing shovel and dig up a couple of nice Christmas trees alongside the track. Putting them securely on the back of the tender, away we would go so that nobody knew what we had been up to.

It was during this time that we both had the great pleasure of being part of the making of the film *Branch Line Railway* with Sir John Betjeman. This was filmed during September 1962 and involved several crews from Templecombe and Highbridge sheds. These included drivers Bert Rendle, Ronald (Chummy) Andrews and George Wheadon. The firemen were Ray Coates and John Rice, along with guard Frank Packer. Also from Evercreech Junction were stationmaster Alec Stowe and foreman John Eaton. The engines used were class 4Fs Nos.44417 and 44560, along with Collett class 0-6-0 Nos.2204, 2277, 3210, 3215 and 3218. During the filming we had an Inspector Arthur McCarthy riding on the footplate with a film crew of two who sat on a couple of beer crates at the back of the tender. They were dressed in overcoats, big glasses and bobble hats to help keep out the draughts and coal smuts from the chimney. Their camera was on a low tripod and tied down with thin wagon rope to secure it in position. On the video Ray and I can be seen at West Pennard, Glastonbury, Aqueduct Crossing and Shapwick.

This was a memorable occasion, but sadly for me and for many others, the S&D has now all gone, all gone.

A silent moment at Pylle as a lone cow grazes on the lush grass. The station looks forlorn and lonely in the distance. There will be no more trains meandering through this station again. (*Eric Rimmer*)

(*left*) Nestling under the A37 road bridge at Pylle is 4F No.44559 with a passenger train from Highbridge in the 1960s. (*John Eaton*)

(*below*) On a bright summer's day we observe Steanbow Crossing, which was situated between Pylle and West Pennard. The signal and gates tell us a train is due. The crossing house still exists and the Dunkerton family are still in residence. (*Ray Dunkerton collection*)

BR class 3 No.82002 with driver Charlie King in charge coasts into Pylle Halt. The signalbox can be seen behind the carriages, with the station house on the right. (*Mike Fox*)

A wonderful bird's eye view on a misty day of West Pennard station. Note the Mini outside the Station House. *(Keith Barrett collection)*

(*above*) With puddles on the platform, and with only a year to closure, 2-6-2T No.41249 heads a train into West Pennard station. (*Paul Strong*)

(*below*) Class 2 No.41214 runs into West Pennard station in the 1960s with a train for Evercreech Junction. The stationmaster's house can be seen on the left-hand side. (*Paul Strong*)

Roy Hix

One day I was working at the Cow & Gate Milk factory at Wincanton with my mate Bill Trigg. We were loading rail trucks with tins of milk powder. S&D shunter Harry Light was on duty and he said: 'Why don't you get a job on the railway, it's a job with a future?' We decided there and then that we would apply for a job and contacted the local shed foreman. After a medical at Eastleigh we were both taken on as engine cleaners. After about 12 months we were made up to passed cleaners which meant that when we were needed we would go onto the footplate and do a firing turn on the main line. After the first couple of trips, we were then called upon to do more and more regular firing turns. I fired to Rodney Scovell, who was a passed fireman at the time and also to Ron Spiller, who was a driver. I recall two stories working with both of them.

I remember one trip with Rodney, when we were returning from Evercreech Junction, having just assisted the Pines Express from Bath. We were now light engine with West Country No.34043, *Combe Martin,* which had an unusual feature, a speedometer. We set sail for Templecombe station where we were to be relieved by a Branksome crew who were going to take her back to Branksome. Rodney said: 'I wonder what speed we can get her up to on the long straight between Wincanton and Templecombe'. Well, the WC had steam-operated gearage and Rodney started notching her up and up. Suddenly she went into a violent shudder, almost going into reverse, he slammed her into low gear which sent the fire out through the chimney. On arrival at Templecombe the Branksome crew were well chuffed, they were an hour late leaving as they had to reinstate the fire. Rodney was not the man of the day with the new crew, who gave him a stiff telling off; this is putting it mildly.

On one winter's night in 1958 I was working with Ron Spiller on a freight train from Highbridge back to Templecombe. On leaving West Pennard we headed for the steep Pylle Bank with a full load of coal and condensed milk from Bason Bridge. We had a 3F Bulldog. Being a wet rail we were using a lot of sand, as the old girl was slipping. Unfortunately we ran out of sand, which meant I had to walk alongside the engine and shovel ballast on to the rails to try to get her to grip. I had just got back on to the footplate to check the boiler when Ron shouted: 'we've broken away'. He jumped off the engine and tried to pin the brakes of the runaway train that was now gathering speed back down the bank; Ron fell over, however, but eventually made his way back onto the footplate. We then tried to decide what to do; having noticed just one truck was still attached to our 3F, Ron said we would go back slowly to West Pennard, shouting out for the guard Ted Scovell (Rodney's father) in case he had jumped the train. However unbeknown to us and Ted, the lady at Cockmill Crossing had phoned the signalman at West Pennard, to say that the train was on its way back. The signalman having heard us struggling up the bank had set the line to the goods siding which was back through the goods shed. Ted, our guard, however, was not prepared for this event, thinking he would run on until it levelled out towards Glastonbury. Unfortunately from the account of the signalman, the train had shot through the goods shed at 50 miles per hour and crashed into the buffers, completely turning Ted's brakevan around blocking the main line. On looking for Ted we eventually found him walking towards Glastonbury, blowing his whistle and completely confused. Although not injured he was a very lucky man to have survived the accident, but he suffered from delayed shock. Coal and tins of condensed milk were everywhere and the passengers who were catching the last branch train of the day from Evercreech had to be taken home by bus. To my recall I am sure Ted never worked on the S&D again. What a night!

***

Two brothers, Billy and Keith Conibeer, also remember this accident, as they were both working on the branch that day as firemen. Keith recalls below the night of the Highbridge Market goods train, as it was called, after it broke away and derailed.

I was on the Highbridge milk train with driver Maurice Cook which left Highbridge about 15.20, picking up milk tanks at Bason Bridge, shunting at Glastonbury and picking up Royal Mail at Templecombe at about 20.15. We were relieved by Templecombe men and then rode back as spare on the cushions to Highbridge. We caught the Bath stopper to Evercreech Junction, and then found out that the last branch train to Highbridge had been cancelled due to the derailment. The engine from it had gone down to West Pennard with driver Bill May and my brother Billy. The Evercreech Junction stationmaster Jack Pike went with them to check the damage. On their return they were relieved by a Templecombe crew. My brother, Bill May, Maurice Cook, myself and our two guards had to find some way to get home from Evercreech. We walked up to the up marshalling yard and caught a goods train to Bath. After getting permission from the guard we all piled into his guard's van. On arrival we all went into the engine shed messroom where we had corned beef and biscuits, which I think came from the emergency breakdown kit, and plenty of tea. After that we all went over to Bath Spa on the Great Western and caught a train to Bristol Temple Meads, then on down to Highbridge, arriving back about 08.15, a very long night. We all turned up for duty later that day.

***

Roy Hix continues:

My recollection of another incident involved a class 7F on a goods train from Hamworthy Docks, near Poole. We were on a night shift starting at 19.00 and made our way down the single-line section to Poole to collect our overnight goods train to Bath. The train was loaded with apples for delivery to Bulmer's Cider Factory at Hereford, the train being made up to a maximum load for a 7F over the steep Mendip Hills. The trucks were not fitted with vacuum brakes which meant the only brakes on the train belonged to the loco and the brakevan. My driver, Peter Guy, was unaware that the guard we had was not familiar with the road to Bath. Also we were not told to stop at Templecombe No.2 signalbox to change over guards. So with no instructions to stop, we came past No.2 and up on to the main line and headed for Evercreech Junction, where a banker was provided for the climb over the Mendips. After the summit at Masbury was reached, the banker left us and went back to the Junction, leaving us to the downhill journey. Passing Chilcompton and Midsomer Norton, little did we know of the next hair-raising experience ahead. The distant signal approaching Radstock was against us, so we started to apply the brakes expecting the guard to do the same with his brakevan. However, by now the weight of the train was increasing our speed to breakneck levels, brakes on the loco were now full on. I had also wound down the tender hand brake

hoping this would help but it made no difference. The brake blocks were red hot and the sparks were flying off the wheels and almost lighting up the sky. Peter pulled the whistle full on and left it on, hoping the signalman at Radstock would open the crossing gates for us to give us a clear run through the station. This was done thanks to Les Willsher, the quick-thinking and observant signalman, as we had just seen the home signal change in our favour. As we thundered over the crossing and through the station, Peter said we had better watch ourselves as we would be into the single line section soon, and into the tunnels with nowhere else to go but the buffers at Bath Green Park. We were hoping that, as all S&D crews knew, the tunnel we were about to enter had a slight incline, and if we could slow her down enough, we could take the rest of the journey into Bath very carefully. Peter was waiting until the last minute, until he could feel the train push back on the engine before setting the brakes on again. Unfortunately the engine stalled; we had come to a stop in Combe Down Tunnel and this meant we had to get the heavy train away on a gradient in the small bore of the tunnel, in which the rails were wet. Sand had to be put on the rails to give us a grip as the engine was now slipping, and with the force of the exhaust rebounding from the tunnel roof, we were covered in red hot cinders cascading down on us. By now we had both put handkerchiefs over our mouths to breathe because of the sulphur in the confined space, but eventually the 7F made her way out of the tunnel and we made a very slow and safe descent into Bath. On arrival, the guard walked down to the engine and was about to ask for a lift back to Wincanton, as we were going back light engine to Templecombe. Peter had some very strong words for him about the lack of co-operation he had given us on the up journey, but Peter soon relented after the guard owned up to not having a clue when or where his brakes had to be applied.

When I look back on my S&D days it is something I will always treasure. Various members of my family have also worked on this railway. My grandmother Maud Hix was the crossing keeper at Horsington Crossing and her husband Samuel was on the permanent way. My brother Alan was a fireman and my uncle Jack was a driver. For me it is hard to believe that the Somerset & Dorset Railway, which my family was a part of, closed 40 years ago. Long live the memory of this railway for generations to come.

(*above*) Looking very smart is guard Ted Christopher with his watch chain prominent. He is carrying his hand lamp and I wonder what is in the wicker basket? (*Mrs. M. Brown collection*)

(*above*) Four S&D railwaymen with many years service between them, are seen here at West Pennard station in the 1940s. From left to right, porter Tom Leonard, driver Ronald Andrews, guard Jack Alford and fireman Alan Jones. (*Barry Andrews collection*)

(*left*) Lying on its side is one of the box wagons mentioned in Roy Hix's memories of the accident which he was involved in at West Pennard in 1958. (*Keith Conibeer*)

(*above*) The crews take a breather at Glastonbury before taking their trains out to Evercreech and Wells, c.1949. Under the footbridge Charlie King looks out of the cab of 1P No.58046 with the stopper from Burnham-on-Sea to Evercreech Junction. The other driver, on another 1P with the Wells train, awaits the green flag to leave the station. (*Keith Barrett collection*)

(⁹⁄₄₁) **SOUTHERN RAILWAY.**
(787)
FROM WATERLOO TO
GLASTONBURY

(*left*) Drifting around the sharp curve and approaching Glastonbury is 7F No.53807 and 4F No.44558 ahead of the Home Counties Railway Society excursion on 7th June 1964. (*Alan Mitchard*)

(*above*) A Scottie goods 0-6-0 No.36 at Glastonbury in 1914. Built by Neilson & Co in 1878 it was withdrawn in 1922. (*Keith Barrett collection*)

(*below*) Seen here on 19 July 1949 at Glastonbury, are driver Ronald Andrews on the platform and fireman Maurice Cook enjoying a rest before taking 0-4-4T class 1P No.1371 back down the branch. (*Barry Andrews collection*)

(*above*) A moment in time at Glastonbury, with guard Jack Alford on the platform and a Morris Commercial LC5 GPO van on the left. Note the rubber front wing. The engine in the background is class 2 No.41283. (*Roger Holmes/Hugh Davies collection*)

(*below*) A busy scene at Glastonbury as driver Les Cuss looks out of the cab of 2219 while parcels are being loaded and unloaded for the trip down the branch to Highbridge. (*David Lawrence/Hugh Davies collection*)

(*above*) With the crossing closed, a scooter on the left sets this 1960s scene at Ashcott station. Closure must be near as the permanent way gang would never let the weeds grow between the sleepers. (*Keith Barrett collection*)

(*below*) In bright sunlight across the grass meadows of Ashcott, a class 2251 No.3210 is seen with a mixed train in 1964. (*Keith Barrett collection*)

(*right*) From the days of handwritten records, 130 years ago, comes this record of a lone parcel sent from Ashcott in January 1876 to Sandford & Banwell on the GWR. (*Paul Strong collection*)

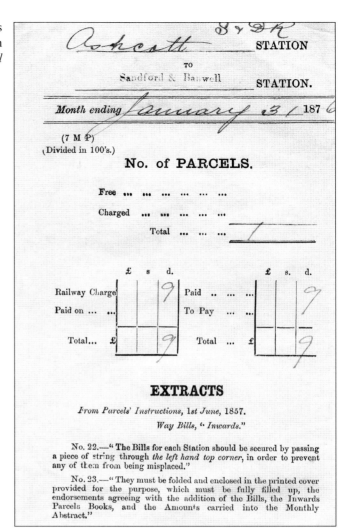

(*below*) In thick fog on 19th August 1949, 0-6-0 No.3260 collided with a narrow-gauge petrol engine hauling peat across the track and ended up in the rhine. Fortunately nobody was hurt. The loco was cut up on site. (*Geoffrey Robinson*)

(*left*) Edna Atwell on the concrete platform with the family's pet cat Winnie. With her husband Archie they ran Ashcott station in the 1960s. (*Janet & Tony Rossiter collection*)

(*below*) Driver George Welch in the cab of GWR Collett class 2251. On the left is the lubricator with the regulator handle across the front. Above is the blower to take away the blowback from the fire. His right hand is resting on the reversing lever, and above fixed in front of the side window is the ATC (Automatic Train Control). (*George Welch collection*)

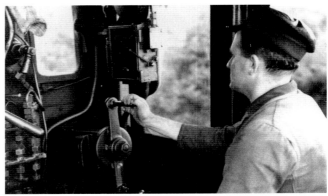

(*above*) A family scene at Ashcott station, with porter Archie Atwell and his wife Edna, with ganger Tom Wall on the right. Note the Standard Ten motor car in the background. (*Janet & Tony Rossiter collection*)

(*right*) Paul Strong had an unusual form of transport to take him to the location of his railway photographs, many of which appear in this book. He is seen here in the 1960s with his 8-wheeled Leyland on a photographing mission on the S&D. His superb pictures will live on as a lovely reminder of past glories on the Somerset & Dorset Railway. (*Paul Strong collection*)

(*above*) It's quiet and peaceful at Shapwick station, with the platform and permanent way looking immaculate. The porter is probably enjoying a yarn and a cup of tea with the signalman in his box. (*Keith Barrett collection*)

(*below*) Shapwick signalman Bill Vowles waiting to exchange tablets with the fireman on class 2251 No.3218 which has made its way from Highbridge. (*David Lawrence/Hugh Davies collection*)

(*left*) Under a lowering sky and looking neglected is class 2251 No. 3210 leaving Edington with a mixed train in 1964. On the left can be seen the *Tom Mogg Inn*. (*Paul Strong*)

(*right*) 3F No. 43682 stands at Edington Burtle station with a local passenger train. A very young fireman can just be seen looking out of the cab. (*Brian Harding*)

(*left*) In October 1964, 0-6-0 No.3218 is about to pass Huntspill Crossing, home to Irene Hynam who worked here for many years. (*Paul Strong*)

(*right*) Most photographs taken at Bason Bridge are seen across the River Brue. It's nice to have this track side shot of Ivatt class 2 No.41296 hauling a rake of milk tanks. (*Roger Holmes/Hugh Davies collection*)

(*left*) A close-up of 4F No.44557, as it is about to leave Bason Bridge for a leisurely stroll across the Somerset levels to its next stop, Edington Burtle. (*Brian Harding*)

(*right*) Footplate crew with driver Charlie King on the right is seen here near Bason Bridge with 3F No.43228 hauling a mixed train. The old 3F could do with a clean. (*G.W. Sharp*)

A view of Highbridge looking east about 1910. An 0-6-0 Scottie is shunting some wagons into the Carriage and Wagon workshop, burnt down in the 1950s. Behind is the Locomotive Works, on the left is the Loco signalbox. In 1948 it was renamed Highbridge East C box. (*SDRT collection*)

(*above*) S&D Johnson 0-4-4T No.55 at Highbridge on the 18.45 Highbridge to Evercreech Junction train in September 1928. (*Jack Hobbs collection*)

(*below*) LMS 0-4-4T No.1346 re-marshalls its train at Highbridge before leaving to travel the branch on 10th June 1935. (*Keith Barrett collection*)

(*above*) Highbridge in the 1920s, with an unidentified Johnson 0-6-0 heading a freight train. What are they burning in the firebox? I hope there are no clothes on any nearby washing lines. (*Jack Hobbs collection*)

(*below*) Fireman Keith Conibeer looking out of the cab of 3F No.43356 at Highbridge Wharf. His brother Billy was also a fireman on the branch. (*Keith Conibeer collection*)

A number of Johnson Tanks on shed at Highbridge on 5 July 1930. No.1202 was built in 1877 as No.12 and No.1305 in 1884 as No.54. (*H.C. Casserley*)

Plenty of activity at Highbridge with two class 2251s. One of them is pulling some milk tanks probably for Bason Bridge. Highbridge East box can be seen above the loco's tenders. The loco in the front, No.2217, has lost its number plate on the side of the cab and the number on the smokebox looks like it has been painted on a piece of wood. (*Paul Strong*)

A fine photograph of Highbridge staff taken in the 1940s. Steamraiser Jim Hayes stands on the buffer of the 3F, on the left, with tube and smokebox cleaner Tom Hardwidge on the right. Sitting down are firemen Les Copper? (left) and Jim Bradner. Standing, from left to right, are driver Stan Bedford, carriage cleaner George Smith, depot foreman Bill Eaton, fitter Cliff Turner and storeman Alan Drew. (*Millbrook House Ltd collection*)

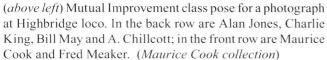

(*above left*) Mutual Improvement class pose for a photograph at Highbridge loco. In the back row are Alan Jones, Charlie King, Bill May and A. Chillcott; in the front row are Maurice Cook and Fred Meaker. (*Maurice Cook collection*)

(*above right*) Highbridge railwaymen on a day out to Bournemouth just after the war. From left to right, foreman Harry Miller, goods guard Frank Salter and drivers George Young, Fred Parsons and Ern Cook. They had over 200 years of service between them. (*Norman Cook collection*)

(*centre right*) Driver Jack Foster (left) and shedmaster Edwin Jackson with the Somerset & Dorset Joint Railway Crest on 29th August 1954 at Highbridge. It is the day after the running of the Centenary of the Somerset Central Railway Special. (*Colin Jackson collection*)

(*right*) The quality of the picture is not ideal, but what a lovely old photograph taken in one of the workshops at Highbridge, c.1900s. Was it taken at Christmas – look at the sign on the wooden panel behind them? (*Barry Andrews collection*)

A lonely sight as driver Ronald Andrews stands next to his engine 3F No.43682 on the turntable at Highbridge. *(R.E. Toop)*

A superb photograph of rebuilt No.17 with a mixed train at Burnham-on-Sea in the late 1800s. (*Keith Barrett collection*)

(*above*) Gricers out in force to welcome a special to Burnham-on-Sea. The motive power is 0-6-0 class 2251 No.3210. I'm sure the residents would love to have their railway back. (*Andrew Ingram collection*)

(*below*) The terminus at Burnham-on-Sea in 1947, with 1P No.1298 blowing off steam. The train formed is the afternoon passenger to Evercreech Junction and Templecombe. (*Keith Barrett collection*)

(*above*) Passed fireman Arthur King is seen leaving his house in Cross Street, Burnham-on-Sea, to book on for a trip down the branch, c.1938. His bike appears to have all the mod cons on it. (*Gordon King collection*)

(*above*) Standing in the cab at Burnham-on-Sea is fireman Ronald Andrews. I wonder who the young lad is with the oil can and also the driver on the platform? (*Barry Andrews collection*)

(*right*) The children of Burnham-on-Sea and Highbridge are standing on 3F No. 43201, which headed the special train that ran from Glaston-bury to Burnham on 28 August 1954 to mark the centenary of the Somerset Central Railway. The footplate crew that day were driver Bill Peck and fireman Maurice Cook. Can anybody recognize themselves? (*Highbridge Social Club collection*)

(*above*) This early view shows the approach to Wells. On the left is the S&D signalbox and in the centre the goods shed. On the right is the loco shed and turning right is Priory Road station. (*Richard Dagger collection*)

(*below*) A very early photograph of SDJR No.53 with three railwaymen on the branch. This engine was built in 1885 and withdrawn in 1930. (*R.K. Blencowe collection*)

(*above*) Johnson 0-4-4T No.58047 approaches Polsham with a short train on the Glastonbury to Wells branch in 1949. (*Joe Moss/R.S. Carpenter collection*)

(*below*) A contractor's diesel locomotive 0-4-0 Planet is seen in use with an ex-GWR bogie bolster C for carrying rails near Cossington on the Bridgwater branch. Bridge No.294, Glastonbury Canal Bridge, can be seen with Edington in the background. (*C.G. Maggs*)

(*below*) The lonely setting of Cossington station with its single platform looking towards Edington Junction. Bridgwater railwayman Will Locke remembers this station well; he recalls one of the porters George Pepperall had a garden opposite the platform and would sell his vegetables to the local villagers. (*C.G. Maggs*)

(*above*) Best clothes are order of the day for a Sunday School outing in 1927. The passengers at Bawdrip Halt are waiting for a train to Burnham-on-Sea for their yearly outing. Looking closely at the photograph they are all wearing hats except for one little boy. (*Will Locke collection*)

(*left*) Carter Edmund White seen here with a parcels delivery horse and cart at Bridgwater. He spent his whole working life on the S&D. (*SDRT collection*)

This photograph is dedicated to the late Will Locke. Will was one of the first S&D railwaymen who gave me a lot of help and advice with my first book, *S&D Memories*. He worked as a porter at Bridgwater North for many years. When the line closed he was devastated. This picture shows Johnson Tank No.58073 with its one solitary coach with the Bridgwater North to Edington train, crossing over the A38 road bridge, Bristol Road, Bridgwater on the last day of passenger service on 29th November 1952. Will was on this train with six other passengers to bid farewell to a line that was his life. (*Douglas Allen*)

40 Years Since Closure

Since the S&D closed in 1966 much has happened. Bridges and viaducts have been destroyed and nearly all the infrastructure of the line has disappeared. This final section is about the groups who are working to keep the memory of the Somerset & Dorset Railway alive. To understand what happened to the S&D after closure, an excellent book, *The Somerset & Dorset (Aftermath of the Beeching Axe)* by Tim Deacon, now sadly out of print, details all that has happened to the line since its demise. As Tim mentions in the preface of the book, he found it a very sad job recording its fate.

In one way or another many hundreds of people have worked tirelessly over the years to remind us of what a marvellous railway it was. I will now hand over to the spokesmen for the four groups.

The Somerset & Dorset Railway Trust

Roy Pitman

The date 7th March 1966 will remain indelibly embedded in the minds of everyone associated in any way with the Somerset & Dorset Railway, employees, passengers and enthusiasts alike. It was the day that the charming line finally closed as a result of the infamous Dr. Beeching's report. No longer would one hear the diddle-ee-dee, diddle-ee-da as the wheels of locomotives and carriages went over the joints in the rails, sounds that had been familiar over many years. No longer would the Mendip Hills ring to the whistles and rattles of trains making their way between Bath and Bournemouth.

Not all was lost as there were many people, from all walks of life, who were determined that at least memories of the Somerset & Dorset Railway would never die. In November 1965, prior to the closure, enthusiasts and devotees met and founded the Somerset & Dorset Railway Circle which later became The Somerset & Dorset Railway Trust. The original intentions were to be an organisation that could be a means of supplying information about the workings and history of the S&D and give members the opportunity to express and exchange views. The station site at Radstock eventually became the headquarters and open days were held, attracting hundreds of interested visitors. It was then possible to have a brakevan ride behind an industrial locomotive a little way up the line as far as the site of Writhlington Colliery sidings.

Then came a change of direction in the aims of the Circle. In 1970, 7F No.53808 was rescued from Barry and brought to Radstock locomotive shed for restoration to running order. Despite many volunteers working hard on the restoration, it was obviously going to be a very long time before the job was completed. When the last of the Somerset coal mines was closed in the mid 1970s, and the Radstock site was to be levelled for future development, the Trust had to vacate their home. They were offered facilities by the West Somerset Railway and Washford was chosen as the new base. Both 53808 and much more other stock and equipment were moved there in 1975. Over the ensuing years a shed and workshop were erected and sidings laid. The old Wells Priory goods office became a messroom and sleeping quarters for the volunteers.

Work continued on the restoration of 53808 but it was eventually practicable to engage the West Somerset Railway to complete all work outstanding to see it back to running order. The big day was on the last Saturday in August 1987 when it hauled a passenger train from Minehead to Bishops Lydeard. On that momentous occasion, there were tears in the eyes of many observers who had waited patiently for the day. Since then it has been withdrawn for renewal of the boiler and a complete overhaul.

Many reunions of ex-S&D staff have taken place at both Bath Green Park and Washford over recent years, providing the opportunity for the employees to reminisce and renew old friendships and for the general public to get the chance to meet and chat to their folk heroes.

The Trust has a thriving membership, produces excellent in-house magazines and books and also has its own internet discussion group. It also has its own sales shop at Washford and online ordering facilities for many S&D items. I was privileged to be

Stationmaster at Washford for 12 years and with the help of my wife Mona and a dedicated band of voluntary helpers it was possible to attract thousands of visitors each year to look around the museum and station site and learn of those wonderful days of the old S&D.

It would be impossible to list the names of everyone who has been a part of the Trust's success, but one person who devoted such an amount of not only his leisure time but also his working life to ensure this success was the late Mike Palmer. He filled almost every office on the committee over the years. Mike is sadly missed and it just isn't possible to replace such a dedicated person.

There is nothing like the sound, smell and sight of a steam engine in action. Once again the Trust's engine, 7F No.53808, is hauling passenger trains, albeit now on the West Somerset Railway, and with this engine in steam, memories of the Somerset & Dorset Railway will never, ever die.

(*right*) Former S&D staff enjoying a reunion at Washford in 1989. On site was 9F No.92220 *Evening Star*. During the day a short service in memory of Ivo Peters was conducted from the footplate.
(*Mona Pitman collection*)

(*above*) An S&D Trust open day at Radstock on 19 September 1971, with Cranford No.2 propelling a brakevan away from the station. (*Ivo Peters, courtesy of Julian Peters*)

Gartell Light Railway

Ian Matthews

It was back in 1984 when John Gartell and his father Alan made a bid for some redundant 2-ft gauge railway equipment from the Fisons Company near Ashcott on the Somerset levels. Their bid for the Lister locomotives was accepted and these were subsequently moved to Common Lane, near Templecombe. The seeds of the Gartell Light Railway were now sown and track and rolling stock soon followed. These Lister locomotives were the first link with the S&D as they were the very locomotives that had hauled trains of peat across the Evercreech to Highbridge line on the levels near Ashcott.

There was never a long-term plan for the railway, it just evolved as John and his father's dream of their very own railway became a reality. As the railway progressed other people became involved and as the line grew longer the S&D trackbed came closer. The trackbed was reached at the old Common Lane level crossing cottage which was occupied by a member of the Gartell family, complete with a replica name board. The new line turned south and headed to Park Lane level crossing, the line's present terminus. Unlike Common Lane, the crossing cottage at Park Lane was demolished by the Gartell family business on closure of the line.

Just south of Common Lane crossing cottage is a completely new station which you will not find on any old S&D map, called Pinesway Junction. The junction is so called because of a further line extending back along the S&D trackbed past the Common Lane crossing cottage, but stopping short of Common Lane.

This line will form part of a future extension north to the outskirts of Templecombe.

Early in 1991 the decision was made to open the G.L.R. to the public; this gave the running of trains a real purpose. It was now possible to travel on the S&D by regular passenger train for the first time since 1966. In June 1998 the diesels were joined by the line's first purpose-built steam locomotive, No.6, called 'Mr. G', after Alan Gartell who had sadly passed away 18 months before. One could now travel by steam-hauled passenger train on the S&D once more.

Although a 2ft gauge railway the G.L.R has very strong links with the S&D. There are three sets of three coaches, coloured Southern green, LMS maroon and S&D blue. The railway has numerous other items of rolling stock including bogie and four-wheeled wagons and a guard's van. The railway is signalled and has two fully operating signalboxes, one being scratch built and the other from Wyke Level Crossing west of Sherborne on the Salisbury to Exeter line. A closer look around the site will uncover other links with the S&D; the concrete lamppost by the water tower is from Station Road, Templecombe, the platform at Park Lane is made up of concrete walkways from Templecombe shunting yard and the catch point sign by Common Lane signalbox is from Templecombe station. The tablet exchange apparatus at Pinesway Junction is from Stalbridge station.

There is a fine restaurant, a picnic area and also a sales shop where there is a good selection of books and other railway items for sale. The G.L.R. opens on Bank Holidays or the last Sunday of each month from Easter to October. It is well worth a visit and you will be sure of a warm welcome.

Steam on the Somerset & Dorset again on the Gartell Light Railway, with No.6, *Mr. G*, climbing up onto the S&D trackbed at Pinesway Junction, heading for Park Lane. In the background can be seen Common Lane Crossing cottage. The track to the right is the start of the northern extension to Templecombe. (*Ian Matthews*)

North Dorset Railway Trust

Mike Rutter

After a speculative advert was placed in a railway monthly in early 1999, a group of people came together in June 1999 to discuss the possibility of preserving Shillingstone station. The venue for this meeting was at *The Silent Whistle* public house next to the station, which has now been demolished and replaced by housing. The purpose of the meeting was to discuss how to prevent such a thing happening to the station, whose survival already owed a lot to good fortune. Shillingstone station is now the only station built by the Dorset Central Railway to survive in Dorset.

A series of events after closure led to this remarkable building surviving into the 21st century. Probably the most important reason for its survival is the fact that the main station building itself was used for small cottage industries. Firstly, and appropriately, it was used for production of kits for railway modellers, and latterly it fell into the hands of furniture makers. From this grew a thriving business and the St Patrick's Industrial Estate grew around the station on the site of the former goods yard. At this time the porters' shed was lost to the developers, the signalbox having been demolished at closure. This left the main station building, parcels office and grain store. The furniture business left the site and the area fell into decline.

The station, along with 1½ miles of trackbed running in a Southerly direction, was purchased by Dorset County Council for use for the proposed Shillingstone Bypass. Because of government cuts it was never built and once again the station survived. Dorset County Council also helped by insisting the industrial estate was not to be redeveloped for housing.

Since the railway's closure, several unsuccessful attempts were made to preserve Shillingstone station, and various traction engine events and tidy-up days were held. The current team involved with its survival first showed interest to D.C.C. in late 1999. Progress was slow and

it wasn't until September 2002 that any advance was made when the owners put the lease up for sale. Thirteen interested parties came forward from which North Dorset Railway Trust was selected, as their proposals best suited the Council's plans for the conservation area that the station now sat in. Because of vandalism and general deterioration of the fabric of the building D.C.C. granted a right of access agreement in November 2003 so that urgent remedial work could take place. Progress has been made steadily ever since, but due to the lack of a completed lease only monies from donations by members of N.D.R.T. were available to finance the restoration. Finally in June 2005 a lease that was acceptable to all parties was signed and was presented to North Dorset Railway Trust by local Conservative MP Bob Walter in a ceremony on the up platform on 22nd July 2005.

With the lease comes the opportunity to apply for grants which will help in the N.D.R.T.'s plans to rebuild the signalbox, porters' shed, down platform shelter, greenhouse and gangers' hut. It is proposed to re-instate the entire railway infrastructure in the leased area, and also construct a restoration building for promotion of heritage skills necessary in the restoration of railway rolling stock. The area will be promoted as a working museum and plans for a picnic area looking over the fine views of the River Stour and Hambledon Hill have been met with enthusiasm.

Preservation started at Shillingstone station in 2005 with the North Dorset Railway Trust. (*Mike Rutter*)

The Somerset & Dorset Railway Heritage Trust

Tim Deacon

Midsomer Norton station is best remembered for its flowerbeds, neat lawns and a greenhouse beside the signalbox, often seen whilst a Jinty shunted coal wagons from Norton Hill Colliery. What a contrast the fledgling Somerset & Dorset Railway Heritage Trust found. None of this survived in 1995 when it first started the restoration. The site was overgrown and the trackbed between the platforms partially in-filled. Two Parks and Gardens department stores covered part of the goods yard, and the exit to the mainline was blocked by tons of soil and rubble.

It is amazing that the station survived at all, when it should have been demolished in 1968 by the contractors lifting the track. By good fortune their contract ended in mid-July 1968, just as track lifting reached the south end of the station. The following spring, after the remaining track down to Radstock had been removed, the station site was taken over by Somervale School. Also at this time the bridge over

Silver Street was demolished and the embankments cut back; much of the rubble and soil was dumped between the station platforms. The station would remain with the Somerset Education department until September 1995 when they sold it to Wansdyke District Council (absorbed into Bath & North East Somerset Council on 1st April 1996).

On 27th March 1996 a three-year lease was signed between Wansdyke Council and the Somerset & Dorset Railway Trackbed Trust, the forerunner of Somerset & Dorset Railway Heritage Trust. This allowed for the repair and restoration of the remaining buildings, but further development such as the reconstruction of the signalbox (largely demolished in the 1970s) and the laying of 1,000 yards of double track and the sidings would require a planning application. Major stepping stones in achieving the Trust's objectives therefore came in late 2001 when full planning permission was granted by Bath & North East Somerset Council; in

Steam back at Midsomer Norton in July 2005 with Jinty No.47493 disguised as 47496 which used to run on the S&D. This photo could have been taken in the 1960s. (*David Neighbour*)

early 2002 when a new 25 year-lease was signed; and in mid-2002 when a Single Regeneration Budget grant triggered rapid progress in restoration and tracklaying.

The long-term objective of the Trust is to return a double-track railway from Midsomer Norton towards Chilcompton. In the short term the plan is to relay double track as far as the in-filled Chilcompton Rock cutting. The station buildings are being restored to show the station close to the way it was in the 1950s, with allowances for modern Health & Safety Rules and access for the disabled. The signalbox is being rebuilt with some original equipment having already been donated, and the greenhouse will be rebuilt in due course. The stable block will become a museum and education centre, holding a database on the S&DJR and local industry, such as Norton Hill Colliery. The station site has already had several visits from local schools. The goods yard has been cleared of its modern day interloper and the sidings relaid and connected to the down mainline. Double track now curves temptingly away from the station towards Chilcompton.

With track relaid the operation of trains will be the lifeblood of the project, and with this in mind the Trust is purchasing suitable rolling stock in keeping with the S&D of the period. A Sentinel locomotive of the type used at Radstock has been acquired and will be restored to full working order. This will perform the necessary shunting within the station area. In July 2005 the first live steam locomotive since March 1966 visited Midsomer Norton station. LMS Jinty No.47493 from the Spa Valley Railway (disguised as 47496, a Radstock engine) was exactly the type of engine that would have shunted Norton Hill Colliery and the station yard in the 1950s. It is hoped in the years to come to have other typical S&D-type steam locomotives visit the station, including one of the remaining S&DJR 7F 2-8-0 freight locomotives. There are also no less than five BR Standard class 9Fs in preservation that worked over the S&D and could visit Midsomer Norton. The only appropriate diesels would be a class 35 Hymek or 08 shunter, used during demolition of the line.

With clear signs in 2005 of the station returning to its former glory and track due to be relaid beyond the original boundary of the site, the membership has now increased to over 500. The Trust's quarterly newsletter, *The S&D Telegraph*, now has the air of a quality product with colour cover and professional layout, allowing its sale at other retail outlets. The Trust can also boast a full sales team for its shop and mail order service.

Contact details for the four groups are as follows:

The Somerset & Dorset Railway Trust
The Railway Station
Washford
Watchet
Somerset
TA23 OPP
Tel: 01984 640869
Website http://www.sdrt.org

Gartell Light Railway
Common Lane
Yenston
Templecombe
Somerset
BA8 ONB
Tel: 01963 370752
Website http://www.glr-online.co.uk

North Dorset Railway Trust
PO Box 88
Shaftesbury
Dorset
SP7 8TF
Website www.shillingstonestationproj.fsnet.co.uk

The Somerset & Dorset Railway Heritage Trust
Midsomer Norton Station
Silver Street
Midsomer Norton
Somerset
BA3 2EY
Tel: 01761 411221
Website www.sdjr.co.uk

Index

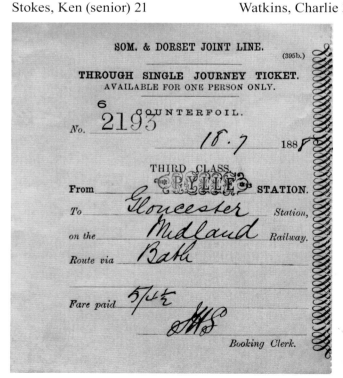

(*left*) A wonderful ticket issued at Pylle in 1888. Note the very fancifully engraved stamp for the station name and elaborate Gothic script initials of the booking clerk. What standards they kept in those days. (*Keith Barrett collection*)

(*above*) An adult and a child ticket for the last passenger train on the S&D, Sunday 6th March 1966. (*Keith Barrett collection*)